ANTIQUE
STYLE

ANTIQUE
STYLE

Rubena Grigg

35 step-by-step period decorating ideas

The Lyons Press

First published in Great Britain in 1999 by Hamlyn
an imprint of Octopus Publishing Group Ltd.

© Octopus Publishing Group Ltd 1999

All inquiries should be addressed to:
The Lyons Press, 123 West 18th Street
New York, NY 10011

A CIP record for this book is available on file

The publishers have made every effort to ensure that
all instructions given in this book are accurate and
safe, but they cannot accept liability for any resulting
injury, damage or loss to either person or property
whether direct or consequential and howsoever
arising. The author and publishers will be grateful for
any information that will assist them in keeping
future editions up to date.

Produced by Toppan Printing Co Ltd
Printed and bound in China

Contents

Introduction

Taste in interior design and style develops and changes over the years. The once-fashionable shiny brocade wing chairs and silky Regency-striped curtains one chose in the 1960s have long since been replaced by linens, slub silks, raw cottons and damasks, luxuriously textured velvets of every type, intensely vibrant silks and soft voiles. Brass bedsteads, four-posters, real linen and antique lace, thickly sumptuous white marcella bedspreads and lovely old quilts and counterpanes, which our grand-parents could not wait to exchange for their modern counterparts, are once again much sought after, and so the wheel keeps turning.

Whether you are fortunate enough to own antiques and family heirlooms or whether you admire period-style interiors and furnishings but do not have the money to spend on antiques or the time to find them, then decorating your home in an antique style provides a pleasurable alternative. We have all been influenced at some time by new trends and different styles – most of us own stripped pine furniture for example. Alternatively, we may feel obliged to hang on to hand-me-downs for sentimental reasons, or to earlier disasters bought out of financial necessity, which now look out of place in their surroundings. Usually, all that is necessary is a little imagination and a pretty paint finish to give such items a new lease of life.

This book is all about creating an effect – linking imagination with a few thrifty inventions to create the look you are aiming for. It is not about antiques. Even the simplest, most informally decorated room can benefit from the clever use of colour and style. *Decorating Tricks Antique Style* offers a huge variety of colourful ideas ranging from the soft neutral hues of old linen and lace used to decorate a small French-style cupboard, to a pretty Victorian bedroom theme in lavender, deep lilac and rose pink, and a vibrant green, reminiscent of verdigris on old copper, painted on an old Singer sewing machine table for an up-to-the minute look.

Most of the pieces of furniture that were bargain buys in this book have been enhanced by adding attractively shaped new backs, angled brackets or skirts, cut in Medium Density Fibreboard (MDF) or wood, with the aid of a jigsaw. Other items have been completely transformed by fitting a new top, mouldings or handles in keeping with the period.

The book is packed with antique-style projects that are grouped in chapters to give a rough indication of the time each project may need (not allowing for drying times of paint or other finishes). If you have a couple of hours to spare, make a blind within an hour from a lovely antique sheet-sham, or give an old galvanized container an attractive verdigris finish. When you have a free evening, transform carved wooden candlesticks into a pair of fabulously opulent silver-gilded candle-holders, fine enough to grace any baronial hall or French *manoir*.

Most of the projects are designed to give wonderful results with the minimum of effort. An inspirational, informative and practical book, it will appeal to anyone interested in creating an antique style and a period mood in their home. The secret of *Decorating Tricks Antique Style* is to recognize the potential in what the majority of people would dismiss as junk and to transform it into something quite spectacular!

Rubena Grigg

Preparation of wood

Unless newly made, most wooden items will be covered with varnish, stain, wax or paint, which may require removal before you can begin work. You could use a professional stripping company to strip a piece of furniture, although there is no reason why most pieces cannot be done by hand. A proprietary stripper, formulated specifically for paint or for varnish, is better than an all-purpose remover. Remove handles, knobs and fittings first, if possible. Always follow the manufacturer's instructions and, if applicable, neutralize any stripper left in the wood with water. Do read the safety precautions and wear thick gloves. Carry out any necessary filling or repairs then, unless the piece is dark stained, treat it as new bare wood (see below) for the purpose of preparation. If you own a power sander, your work will be cut by half.

STAINED WOOD

Sand the stained surfaces with medium-grade sandpaper, always working in the same direction as the grain in the wood.

Wood stain "bleeds" into any paint applied on top so a barrier has to be created between the two, which is why shellac varnish is necessary. Coat the item with shellac, which has been thinned a little with methylated spirits (called denatured alcohol in the USA). Shellac varnish is fast drying and it should be possible to apply a second coat within half an hour. Keep your brush soft in the meantime in a little methylated spirits in a glass jar – not plastic which would disintegrate. When the shellac varnish is dry, paint the item in the normal way with acrylic primer undercoat, followed by a top coat of emulsion paint, both of which are water-based paints.

BARE WOOD

Run your fingers over the surface of the wood to find any particularly rough patches and rub them down with medium-grade sandpaper, again always working in the same direction as the grain in the wood. Remove the dust and, if there are any knots in the wood, apply sanding or knot sealer.

Next, apply the first coat of acrylic primer undercoat, which frequently requires thinning with a little water so that it brushes on more easily. Allow the paint to dry before sanding the whole piece again, using a fine sandpaper, paying particular attention to any edges. Remove the dust and apply a second, slightly thinned coat of primer undercoat. Let it dry.

Apply a third coat if necessary, but if the piece now looks fine in its undercoat, apply sufficient coats of top colour – matt, vinyl silk or soft sheen emulsion paint, or another water-based paint – for a dense all-over cover.

MEDIUM DENSITY FIBREBOARD (MDF)

Always remove the surface dust before painting MDF. Then thin some acrylic primer undercoat paint with a little water before applying the first coat. Let the paint dry. Using fine sandpaper, sand the entire surface of the MDF, paying particular attention to any mouldings which will have roughened up again with the application of paint. Remove the dust and apply another coat of acrylic primer undercoat. Leave to dry. Give the surface a second fine sanding. If it requires another coat, paint it again but there is no need to sand again. It is now ready for the top coat of water-based paint.

PAINTED SURFACES

If the painted surface is even and you intend repainting the item, use a medium-grade sandpaper to rub down the entire surface, always working in the same direction as the grain in the wood. This will create a good "key" on which to repaint.

Remove dust with a damp cloth or vacuum cleaner, before beginning to paint. First, apply two coats of acrylic primer undercoat, which has been slightly thinned with water, letting the first coat dry, before applying the second. When dry, feel the surface by running your fingers over it. Sand down any rough patches with fine sandpaper, paying particular attention to the edges of tops and drawers, for example. Apply two or three coats of top colour in a water-based paint.

Decorative finishes

Excluding the fabric ideas, all of the projects in this book involve the use of paint to some extent. Certain projects use metallic waxes, also known as gilt creams, and others include decoupage techniques – all of these products and techniques create stunning decorative finishes. With regard to paint finishes, some of the major paint manufacturers supply emulsion paint in small tester tins (8fl oz/250ml), which are ideal for many of the projects in this book. These tester tins provide you with small amounts of paint – often all that is needed – and they are available in literally hundreds of exciting colours at relatively low cost.

Artist's acrylic tube paint can be mixed with emulsion paint to alter the colour slightly: to strengthen it or to deepen or lighten the shade. The two mediums work well together. If you already have white emulsion paint in matt, vinyl silk or soft sheen, use it to dilute acrylic tube paint or mix it with the acrylic paint to create the desired shade. This is a less expensive option than using a lot of acrylic paint, especially for mixing emulsion glazes. As long as they are all water-based, paints can be mixed and matched together.

Artist's acrylic paint comes in two popular sizes, but is usually available to order in larger amounts. In addition to specialist suppliers, good stationers often stock artist's materials. For painting furniture and for decorating tinware and other items, it is best not to dilute the acrylic paint too much. When the mixture is watery the paint tends to spread and lose its definition.

SPONGING

Many of the paint finishes in the book have been accomplished using a natural sea sponge. For a lovely, soft emulsion paint glaze, use equal parts of PVA glue and emulsion paint, mixed 1:4 with water. This glaze is a low-odour, fast-drying medium, which keeps well in a screw-top jar or airtight container. The various "recipes" for paint glazes throughout the book suggest using artist's acrylic tube paints or, alternatively, small amounts of matt emulsion paint.

They can be used together, but if you can find the required colour in a ready-mixed form, you may as well use it in the glaze since it is less costly, and means that you will have some glaze leftover for future use.

On the Regency Desk (see page 126) and the Enamel Towel Holder and Soap Dish (see page 68), I used the sea sponge loosely open so that its subtly coloured shape and pattern became the design on the surface of the work. In the other projects I

squeezed the sponge up a little in the hand and dabbed closely to give a flowing movement on the surface, a technique that I call "close-sponging". The faux marble finish on the Singer Sewing Machine Table (see page 118), as well as the parchment finish on both the Edwardian Ewer and Bowl (see page 82) and the Edwardian Washstand (see page 132), were applied in this way. Sponging can be as sparse or as "busy" as you wish, but should never be regimented.

Look at any door panel and you will notice that often only two, or possibly three, sides of the wooden surround are visible. Copy the effect in your painting by shading two edges – one side and the bottom perhaps – and where applicable highlighting the others. It is important always to differentiate between the shadows which describe or depict the shape of an object and the shadows that the object casts.

TROMPE L'OEIL

The idea of trompe l'oeil is to give a three-dimensional effect which deceives the eye into believing it is the real thing, and highlighting and shading are part of this trick. To be a real trompe l'oeil artist capable of painting landscapes and figures and amazing views disappearing into the distance, one has to be confident in the art of perspective. However, in its most basic form, using shadows and highlights to make the painted image look three-dimensional, and for depicting mouldings, frames, panelling, carving and columns, for example, it is both astonishingly successful and realistic, as well as simple to achieve.

WAXES

Waxes are used for a whole range of effects, such as patinating, antiquing, liming and verdigris – many examples of which are in this book. There is a huge range of products now available (like the recommended Liberon range), which have been formulated to enable the home decorator to

reproduce similar look-alike finishes of every kind, including metallic. The new imitations cannot be compared with the real thing – metallic paints, powders and waxes will never have the reflective brilliance, depth or beauty of silver and gold leaf and real gilding, but they can help you achieve the *effect*.

Metallic waxes, also known as gilt creams, are some of the quickest and easiest products to use. They can be brushed on densely (see Tripod Lamp, page 32), or rubbed sparingly over

colour for highlighting areas (see Pot Pourri Holders, page 42).

GOLD AND SILVER LEAF

For the inexperienced and amateur gilder (like myself), Dutch metal leaf laid on to a water-based gold size is the simplest method of gilding. The gold size is painted on to the preferably smooth surface of the item to be gilded and must be left for at least 15 minutes, preferably longer, before the leaf is applied. It is fast drying, and certainly after 24 hours at the most, can be sealed or antiqued, as you like. Real gold never tarnishes, but Dutch metal must be sealed to prevent discoloration.

Gilding with transfer leaf (real gold or silver) or the more inexpensive Dutch metal leaf gives a much richer and more intensely lustrous finish than that given by metallic waxes, gold paint, liquid leaf or metallic powders. If you prefer a slightly softer appearance, new gilding can be antiqued and distressed.

Antique finishes

All of the ageing and antiquing techniques in the book are designed to give an item a slightly worn look, which suggests both the effects of time and the collection of dust and dirt that would have naturally occurred over the ages. To a novice decorator, as I recall vividly, it seems a strange thing to cover a smart, newly painted piece with dirty brown liquid or wax! The beauty of antiquing, however, is that it tones down the newness of the paint, giving it a softer, more mellow appearance, which helps an otherwise new item blend in more readily with the old.

ANTIQUING LIQUID

The most common and effective method of giving an item an antique finish is to mix up an antiquing liquid, as follows.

You will need

*Artist's oil tube paint in
    raw umber
Jam jar with lid
White spirit
Small brush to mix
1in (2.5cm) household
    paintbrush
Kitchen paper*

1. Squeeze out about 1in (2.5cm) of raw umber oil tube paint on to a jar lid. Add a small amount of white spirit to it. With the small brush, mash the paint into the liquid thoroughly.

2. Scrape the oily mixture into the jar. Add another two or three tablespoons of white spirit and mix well.

3. Paint this on to the piece of furniture, beginning in a less conspicuous area until you are more confident. Starting at the top, brush on the antiquing liquid in the direction of the grain. Do not worry when it runs into every crevice, nook and cranny – that is the idea. Leave for 5 minutes.

4. Next remove any surplus antiquing liquid from the painted decoration. Using plenty of kitchen paper, wipe the liquid from the surfaces, working in the direction of the grain, until the paper is almost clean.

5. The depth of antiquing is simply a matter of personal taste.

Even if you wipe an item almost clean of the antiquing liquid, the colour will have mellowed at least. If you have a disaster when applying the antiquing liquid, you can remove it with neat white spirit.

EMULSION WASH

For an opaque, dusty appearance, simply cover painted surfaces with a thin wash of emulsion paint diluted 1:4 with water. A number of brown tones can be used – a coffee-coloured liquid is a good colour to use.

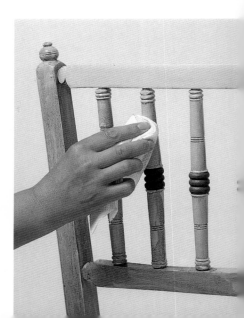

WAX

Waxed surfaces can be buffed up and highly polished to a wonderful antique patina. Beeswax polish can be coloured with artist's oil tube paints – it smells lovely and acts as a protective covering. It will need redoing every now and again to improve both the shine and the protection provided by the wax.

ANTIQUE AND CRAQUELURE FINISH

Crackle varnish is sold as a pack or kit, containing two bottles of varnish, which interact to produce a fine web of almost invisible fissures or cracks. The first to be applied is the darker and slow-drying oil-based ageing varnish; the second is a brittle fast-drying, water-based varnish. The process is often unpredictable, however, and it is recommended that you test it in your own environment before applying it to your masterpiece.

You will need

Two-part craquelure kit
1in (2.5cm) household
paintbrush
Washing-up liquid
Hairdryer
Small brush to mix
Artist's oil tube paint in
raw umber
White spirit
Kitchen paper
Good-quality semi-matt oil-
based varnish or
polyurethane lacquer

1. Apply an even coat of the oil-based ageing varnish sparingly to your chosen item.

2. Allow this to dry for at least 4–6 hours, when it may feel tacky, or overnight when it will feel dry. The time will vary according to room temperature and to how thickly it is painted on. The drier the tack, the smaller the eventual cracks will be – if it is too dry there will be no cracks at all!

3. Next, apply the water-based crackle varnish sparingly. At this stage small bubbles will appear, giving the surface almost a foamy look, and it may be difficult to eradicate the brushstrokes. To overcome this, there is an excellent tip (passed on to me by Belinda Ballantine). Put the brush down and gently massage the surface with the flat sides of your fingers. This helps the top coat to adhere well before it dries, counteracting air bubbles and brush marks. Hold the item to the light if possible so that it reflects on the surface. If you can still see brush marks or "holes", dip a fingertip into a drop of washing-up liquid and massage that into the top coat before it dries – you will find this works wonders.

4. Leave for at least 1 hour or, better still, overnight. Then apply extra warmth from a hairdryer set to warm – not hot, otherwise the varnish will blister! Take time to blow it over the surface, the cracks may not happen instantly so be patient! They are quite difficult to see.

5. Mix raw umber oil tube paint with a little white spirit to the consistency of toothpaste and rub it into the whole of the cracked surface, using kitchen paper or a small paintbrush.

6. When the surface is covered, wipe off the excess paint with clean, dry kitchen paper, pushing the colour into the cracks. Continue until the paper is clean – working in a circular motion. For larger areas, complete a section at a time.

7. Leave at least overnight for the oil paint to dry. It must then be sealed with oil-based varnish, because the cracked surface is water soluble, and therefore must not come into contact with moisture or water before it has been sealed. Use a semi-matt vanish which will take off the unattractive shine on the surface.

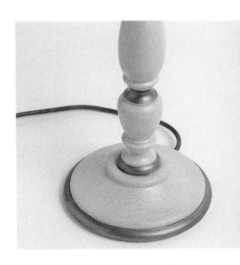

Basic equipment

Whether you intend working on a piece of furniture at ground level, or on a table or work surface, begin by spreading out dust sheets or medium-duty clear polythene (available by the length from decorating shops or do-it-yourself suppliers). Gather together a few miscellaneous tools necessary for the project in hand: an old screwdriver to open paint tins, old spoons for measuring paint, kitchen paper, gloves, jam jars, a straight edge if necessary (a piece of picture moulding will do) and a container of water handy for diluting paint and keeping brushes and sponges soft while you are working.

BRUSHES AND SPONGES

Household paintbrushes – For most projects use a 1in (2.5cm) medium-quality household paintbrushes that will not shed many hairs when used for painting and varnishing.
It is advisable to keep separate brushes for working with oil-based and water-based products and for paints and varnishes. Brushes with man-made bristles or hairs work well with acrylic water-based paints.

After using varnish and paint, make sure you always wash brushes out with the appropriate solvent to avoid ending up with solid brushes which can no longer be used. When using acrylic-based products, the brush can be left in a small amount of clean water in between using, but should be washed out in warm soapy water before being rinsed thoroughly and left to dry. If hairs protrude, wrap the brush in kitchen paper to reshape. If you are using an oil-based paint, varnish or polyurethane lacquer, you will need to clean your brush thoroughly in white spirit, before washing it in warm soapy water.

Artist's paintbrushes – Artist's paintbrushes made from man-made fibres are best suited for applying antique gold on to mouldings, for painting bows, ribbons and leaves and other work involving the use of acrylic gold paint. They are reasonably priced and are ideal for this task, since the gold sediment will eventually clog up the ferrule, separating the hairs and ruining the brush. Sable brushes are far too soft and expensive for this type of work. Artist's paintbrushes nos. 1, 2 and 3 are suitable for painting fine detail, nos. 4 and 5 are good for painting the body of flowers and so on, and for applying antique gold acrylic paint to the rims of jugs and bowls and for mouldings on smaller items. Nos. 7 and 8 are suitable for painting large mouldings – on chair legs and tables, or for filling in areas like the border of the French Cupboard (page 46), or for painting the blue bow and mouldings on the Edwardian Dressing Table (page 100)

Fitches – Round fitches are the most versatile of all the fitches, having a high bristle count and therefore holding a larger quantity of paint. They are available in different qualities – inexpensive round fitches were used for the projects in the book.

Lining brush, or "coachliner" – Available from artist's suppliers, a lining brush has very long hairs which make it much easier for painting either a straight line or a long even curved line. You need to ensure that you load the brush evenly with paint.

Natural sea sponges – Although it is now frowned upon to collect natural sea sponges, it is not possible to achieve the right effect for the paint finishes in this book using a man-made equivalent. Baby sponges are adequate for using on a piece of furniture or small items and are reasonably priced. To decorate a wall, however, you will need to use a larger sea sponge, available from some of the specialist suppliers listed in the Directory of Suppliers on page 140.

ABRASIVES

Sandpaper is a general term commonly used for abrasives. The brown sheets of "sandpaper" normally found in hardware shops are in fact glass papers, which are really only suitable for preparing new wood, but they are frequently all that is available. Other abrasives include garnet paper (sometimes called cabinet paper), silicon carbide paper, flour paper and aluminium oxide paper.

Abrasives are graded by their grit size, which is marked on the back of each sheet – the lower the number the coarser the grade. Three grades are probably sufficient for preparing something from the raw timber stage, for example 100, then 180 and lastly 240 grade for finishing. A 100 grade is good for sanding wooden furniture in its stripped or raw state (or for sanding old paintwork in order to make a "key" over which to repaint). When the first coat of an acrylic primer undercoat is dry the piece can be sanded with 180 grade before applying a second coat. When the last undercoat is dry 240 grade can be used for the surface and all the edges to create a silky finish.

Aluminium oxide "wet and dry" paper is black in colour and the finest of all papers. The 1000 grade is used for sanding the water-based lacquered surface on decoupage, only after at least ten coats have been applied – preferably many more. Use it with a small amount of water and remove the powdery liquid by wiping with a damp cloth until perfectly clear. Dry the surface and wipe with a tack cloth before applying more lacquer.

DECOUPAGE EQUIPMENT

Paper cut-outs – Good-quality wrapping paper with plenty of definition, prints, hand-coloured photocopies or colour photocopies can all be used for decoupage. It is essential that the paper is printed on one side only, otherwise the pattern on the reverse will show through when you apply the varnish. If you are using a mixture of papers, they must be the same type – whether photographed, hand-painted or printed – otherwise they will look illogical and ill matched. They also need to be of the same grade of paper, i.e. thickness.

Scissors – Use small, pointed and very sharp scissors for decoupage. It is a matter of preference whether you use straight or curved scissors. You should not use a scalpel or craft knife because these will scuff the edges of the paper and make incisions which are too angular. They are also much slower to use than scissors.

Glue – You will need water-soluble, ready-mixed heavy-duty wallpaper paste and a small pasting brush. Wallpaper paste is my own preference – I have tried using PVA glue, but find that it is incompatible with the paint-finished background which is often an emulsion glaze, made up of PVA glue, emulsion paint and water. Wallpaper paste is hard-wearing and much easier to use. Remember never to touch your face with sticky fingers since most wallpaper pastes contain fungicide which can irritate the skin.

Cleaning materials – Use a small sponge or sheets of kitchen paper, dampened slightly with water, to clean off excess paste from your work. A tack cloth is a varnish-impregnated cloth used for removing dust particles from items before each coat of varnish is applied. There are several good brands on the market.

Lacquer and varnish – A water-based acrylic lacquer has been specifically formulated for decoupage. You will need to apply ten coats, allow to dry and then rub down with 1000 grade aluminium oxide paper, used wet (see above). Decorator's acrylic varnishes are unsuitable for decoupage, as they become milky and rubbery in appearance.

The wonderful thing about water-based lacquer is the fast drying time, allowing many coats to be applied in one day. Also, it does not alter the background colour of the piece, as the oil-based varnishes do. It will, however, never look the same as oil-based varnish; nor does it have the fabulous depth of the latter. The trick, therefore, is to use perhaps ten coats of water-based lacquer, before moving on to a good-quality semi-matt oil-based varnish (such as Mylands No 8 semi-matt, sometimes labelled semi-gloss!). Always remember to use the tack cloth to remove dust from the surface before each coat of varnish. Leave the varnish or lacquer to dry out completely before applying another coat. (Note; the common term "varnish" or "varnishing", in this case also applies to lacquer and lacquering.)

Other accessories – You will need a suitable board on which to paste glue on to the cut-outs. A piece of Formica, white-faced hardboard or the smooth side of ordinary hardboard – all available from building suppliers or do-it-yourself stores – or stiff card or heavy-duty polythene are all suitable as pasting boards.

A craft knife is useful for lifting pasted cut-outs from the board or for adjusting their position on the surface of your work. Chalk is useful for drawing around the shape of the cut-out design and, finally, screw-top jars or clean plastic containers with lids (such as margarine tubs or ice-cream cartons) make ideal receptacles for paint, glazes and water. (Note: always store solvents in glass containers.)

One-hour wonders

Combine imagination with a few thrifty inventions to create the look you are aiming for. Utilize fabric remnants to add a splash of colour while linking together odd pictures, or hang crisp white antique linen and lace at the windows for dazzling effect. Give a galvanized planter an antique verdigris finish or transform a white plastic container into a "lead" urn and match it up with a "medieval" corbel to make a real impact in a courtyard or garden.

Picture bows

Introducing a picture bow in an eye-catching colour is an ideal and easy way of brightening up a dull corner anywhere in your home. Fabric in soft and subtle colours blends beautifully with antique frames, old watercolours, sepia photographs and prints, while rich and vibrant colours reflect the light and draw the eye.

PINK SILK BOW

You will need

20 x 11in (51 x 28cm) rectangle of pink silk for the bow, plus 12 x 3in (30 x 7.5cm) strip for the tail
Iron
Pins
Sewing machine
Tape measure
Matching thread and needle
1in (2.5cm) curtain ring

Picture bows are equally effective used on a simple whitewashed wall or against strong earthy pigments or dark moody tones.

If you have mixed and matched fabrics as part of your room's colour scheme, you may have leftover checked, striped or plain fabric which could be used for picture bows. Most shops sell small remnants and offcuts at a reasonable price. Two yards (2m) is usually the minimum amount of fabric accepted as an order, but you may wish to cover a chair seat or stool or make cushions to add colour and style to the room, which would leave you with sufficient fabric for making picture bows.

1. Take the large rectangle of pink silk and fold it in half lengthways, right sides together. Press gently, using the iron on a silk setting.

2. Pin the silk in place to stop it from slipping while sewing. Machine stitch ½in (1.5cm) from the edge of the fabric around three sides of the rectangle, leaving one short side open.

3. Turn the stitched rectangle of fabric the right side out; tuck in the raw edges of the unstitched short side of the rectangle and press to hold the raw edges in place.

4. With the rectangle positioned horizontally in front of you, fold both short ends inward so that they meet in the centre and pin them in place. Machine stitch the ends down, stitching fairly close to the edges of the fabric but turning the sewing line before reaching the ends.

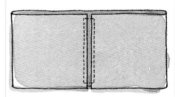

5. Fold the smaller piece of silk in half lengthways, right sides together, and press as you did for the first piece of silk. Pin and machine stitch along three sides of the rectangle, as before.

6. Turn the fabric the right side out, tuck in the raw edges of the unstitched short side, press and machine stitch on top as before to close the opening.

7. Position the first piece of silk, with the machine stitching uppermost, horizontally across the second piece, about 2½–2¾in (6.5–7cm) down from the top of the tail – this is the end with the visible stitching.

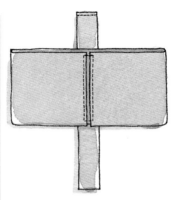

8. Fold over the top of the tail and wrap it around the middle of the bow, while gathering up the bow in the middle.

9. Hand sew firmly at the back to secure the bow, at the same time stitching in place the curtain ring, which is for hanging the bow on the wall.

10. Thread the end of the tail through the ring or D-shaped

17

fitting on the back of the picture frame and hand sew in place to secure the picture to the fabric. Alternatively, hang the bow on the wall, position the picture below it and tap the picture pin through the tail of the bow.

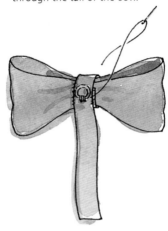

LONG-TAILED ROSETTE WITH TASSEL ENDS

You will need

*Pins, including a long glass-
    or bead-headed pin
Two 26 x 3in (66 x 7.5cm) strips
    of pink silk for the rosette
Sewing machine
Iron
Matching thread and needle
Scissors
40 x 3½in (102 x 9cm) strip of
    green silk moiré for the
    rosette, plus four 24 x 3in
    (61 x 7.5cm) strips for
    the tails
2 small key tassels
Circular back from a small
    rosette tassel or 9in
    (23cm) narrow cord coiled*

*into a circle, with the ends
    hidden and the coil
    secured with stitches
1in (2.5cm) curtain ring*

The size of this long-tailed rosette makes it ideal for dressing large pictures and it would look appropriate in a formal setting or in a high-ceilinged room where pictures may be hung in a higher position or on a picture rail.

1. To make the outer circle of the rosette, pin the right sides of the two pink strips together. Machine stitch ½in (1.5cm) from the edge around three sides, leaving one short side open. Turn the right side out. Tuck in the raw edges of the unstitched side, press and machine stitch on top to close.

2. Starting at the other end of the pink strip, begin folding the now double thickness fabric into

small pleats to form a circle. Hand sew in position as you go with small stitches at the back, and secure the front folds with two or three stitches around the centre, which will be hidden later.

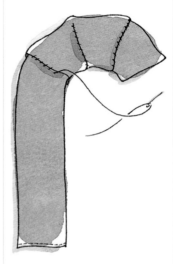

3. Continue until you have a circle; finish by securing the end of the pink strip across the hole in the middle of the circle, to which the rest of the rosette can be attached later.

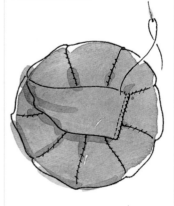

4. Take the single long strip of green silk moiré; turn under ½in (1.5cm) along the long edges and press. Fold the fabric in half

lengthways, wrong sides together, and press.

5. Using thread doubled for strength, secure the thread well at one end of the fabric by oversewing a few stitches then sew the long edges of the green silk together, using a loose running stitch.

6. Draw the fabric along the thread to gather it; the long band will begin to curl around into circles. Secure the loose ends of thread temporarily by wrapping them in a figure of eight around a long glass- or bead-headed pin stuck in the gathered fabric, which will hold the green rosette in place until it is hand sewn on to the pink outer circle of the rosette.

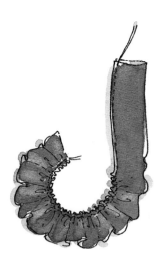

7. Form the gathered fabric into two or three circles, place it on the pink circle and fix firmly with stitches, out of sight and at the back, sewing through all the layers and neatening the ends.

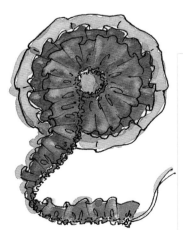

8. Cut a "V" shape at one end of each of the four green strips for the tails. Sew the pairs of lengths together to make the two tails, following the instructions for Step 1, leaving the short straight ends unstitched. Turn the tails the right side out; finish the ends by tucking, pressing and machine stitching on top as before.

9. Attach the cord top of the key tassels to the V-shaped ends of the tails by carefully hand sewing through only one layer of the fabric, so that the stitches do not show on the front.

10. Lastly, hand sew the back of the rosette tassel or the coiled circle of cord to the centre of the rosette, and sew the top of the tails to the back of the rosette. Sew the curtain ring on to the back of the tails and hang the rosette on the wall.

11. Position the picture in place below it and tap the picture pin through the tails of the rosette.

STRIPED COTTON BOW

You will need

*Two 44 x 3in (112 x 7.5cm)
    strips and two 16 x 3in
    (40.5 x 7.5cm) strips of
    pink striped cotton for
    the tails; plus two 18 x 5in
    (46 x 13cm) strips for
    the bow*
Iron
Scissors
Pins
Sewing machine
Tape measure
Matching thread and needle
1in (2.5cm) curtain ring

The long striped cotton bow is young and fresh in its appeal and would be perfect in a bedroom or

a child's room. It is particularly useful for grouping together three or four small pictures of a similar size to make a feature.

1. Fold all four tail pieces in half lengthways, right sides together. Press then cut across one end of each piece at an angle to give the tails shaped ends. Pin in place then machine stitch ½in (1.5cm) from the edge of the fabric around the long sides and the short angled end of each piece.

2. Turn the four tails the right side out, tucking in the raw edges on the unstitched ends. Press then machine stitch these closed.

3. To make the bow, pin the two remaining strips of cotton, right sides together. Machine stitch around three sides and complete the piece, following Steps 3 and 4 of the Pink Silk Bow (see page 17).

4. Assemble the bow and tails as for the Pink Silk Bow, laying the bow horizontally across the two longest tails with one tail top extended slightly beyond the other so that only one folds down over the bow – this reduces the bulk around the bow.

5. Hand sew the two shorter tails and the curtain ring to the back of the bow.

6. Hang the bow on the wall. Position the pictures in place below it, tapping the picture pins through the longest tails.

Summer blinds

Try creating a light and airy fresher look in your home during the summer months.
A crisp white antique sheet-sham or a beautiful lace tablecloth as a half blind at a
window behind curtains provides some privacy and creates a wonderful dappled light.

**ANTIQUE SHEET-SHAM
BLIND**

You will need

Expandable curtain rod
Sheet-sham

Simple lace panels, bedspreads or tablecloths all make ideal window dressings. Experiment by hanging a lovely old white lace panel or a fine antique linen and lace bedspread on simple metal clips that slip on to the curtain pole. It can be pulled to one side during the daytime and drawn across at night with the windows open to let in the air.

Look out for beautiful lace-edged sheet-shams in antique markets. Sheet-shams saved having to wash sheets too often and were attached by buttons (the buttonholes are in the sham) and therefore easily removed for laundering. In this way the turned out decorative part of the sheet always looked good.

Alternatively, make your own blind, remembering to allow for a heading through which to slot the curtain rod, and add wide crocheted or knitted lace.

Expandable curtain rods cover a variety of widths – 4–7ft (1.22–2.13m) for instance – since the pole is easily adjusted by simply tightening a screw. Choose one suitable for the size of your window and follow the fitting instructions on the pack.

1. Simply push the curtain rod through the existing heading in the sham and hang it up (see diagram, top)! If your sheet-sham does not have an opening at the ends of the "heading", a seam here would probably be difficult to unpick since the fabric has been well starched over the years. If this is the case, make a neat cut in the back of the heading through which to slot the pole. The starch in the fabric means this small nick is unlikely to fray.

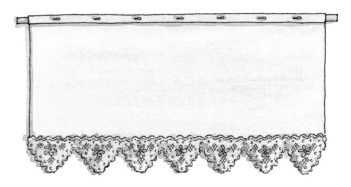

TABLECLOTH BLIND

You will need

Linen and lace tablecloth
Expandable curtain rod

1. If you are buying a lace tablecloth to use as a blind, bear in mind the width of your window since the cloth is folded over the curtain rod. If the cloth is to hang behind curtains and the sides are therefore out of view, it can be a little too narrow, but too wide a tablecloth would be a problem.

This blind is probably best at the top of the window frame, (see diagram, bottom) unless you have very long sash windows in which case you have a choice.

Verdigris galvanized planter

Real verdigris is a bluey-green coating which forms on copper and copper alloys when the metals are exposed to damp. Recreating the effect gives an attractive antique quality and a weathered appearance to ordinary metal objects such as this old galvanized container, now used as an eye-catching planter.

You will need

Scrubbing brush or scourer
Galvanized container
Hot water and washing-up liquid
1in (2.5cm) household paintbrush
Matt emulsion paint in green
Fitch
Liberon verdigris wax

There are expensive kits available on the market which you can use to achieve a verdigris look, but the matt emulsion paint and verdigris-tinted wax used here can do the trick in minutes for next to nothing. This simple verdigris finish not only adds colour to an item but also enhances an imperfect surface.

As an alternative to displaying your verdigris planter outside, potted with plants like the colourful geraniums shown here, you could use the container decoratively inside the house. Fill it with delicate dried rose buds or with a sculptural arrangement of long-stemmed dried lavender tied upright in a sheaf surrounded by lichen.

Put the container outside again in the spring and fill it with composted soil. Plant it with nasturtium seeds and watch them climb everywhere, their vibrant splash of colour brightening up a courtyard or corner of the garden.

1. Using a stiff brush or a good scourer, scrub the galvanized container well using plenty of hot water and washing-up liquid. Rinse well and leave it to dry thoroughly.

2. Place only the very tip of the household paintbrush into the green emulsion. Stipple the paint on to the galvanized surface in patches, applying it to the outside of the container and for about 6in (15cm) down on the inside. Allow the paint to dry.

3. Using a fitch, stipple on the verdigris-tinted wax, again applying it in patches. Use the wax all over the outside of the container and inside at the top, allowing the painted green background to show through in places to give the greenish mottled effect. Leave the wax to set. When dry, the container is ready for use.

Medieval urn & corbel

Painted to look as though they are made of lead, this authentic-looking corbel is in fact concrete and the urn is made of lightweight plastic! Quick and easy to transform, they provide unusually attractive focal points for a garden, courtyard or hall.

LEAD URN

You will need

Plastic urn
Matt emulsion paint in black or dark grey, cream and brown (optional)
1in (2.5cm) household paintbrushes
Old spoon and plate
Talcum powder
Exterior matt varnish

1. Paint the urn, both inside and out, with black or very dark grey emulsion. Leave the paint to dry.

2. Before applying a second coat of paint, turn the urn upside down and cover any overlooked areas. Ensure the urn has a good dense covering of paint all over.

3. Spoon a small amount of the different paints on to your "palette". Add a little talcum powder to the cream emulsion to add texture. Using just one brush and moving from colour to colour, dip it into the different colours and roughly stipple on the paint. Use the darkest colour where there would naturally be shade and stipple lighter colour on to the raised surfaces to highlight them. Do not try to clean the brush between colours since a much better effect will be achieved by blending all the colours. Allow the paint to dry for a short while before going over it again to get the look you want, then leave until completely dry.

4. To finish the urn seal the paint with two coats of exterior varnish – otherwise the paint will eventually peel off – allowing the first coat to dry thoroughly before applying the second.

MEDIEVAL CORBEL

You will need

Old spoon
Matt emulsion paint in black or dark grey, white or cream and dark brown
Plastic carton with lid
1in (2.5cm) household paintbrush
Concrete corbel
Exterior matt varnish (optional)

Although an architectural salvage yard may yield an original corbel, you can easily make your own. Decorative corbels and sconces are enjoying a popular revival, made in wood, metal, plaster, stone, resin, plastic and even polystyrene! The trick is in the finish – making it so convincing that the piece looks authentic.

1. Transfer three or four tablespoons of black or dark grey emulsion paint to a plastic carton. Add a little white or cream and stir, mixing it in well to a dark lead-like grey colour.

2. Paint the uppermost surface of the corbel; leave the paint to dry. If the concrete is particularly porous, repeat the process with another coat or two, until the surface begins to fill up with the paint and has a smoother finish.

3. Turn the corbel over and repeat the process.

4. When you are satisfied with the finish and the painted corbel is completely dry, replenish the lead-grey paint in the base of the carton. Use the carton lid as a palette and place on it a spoonful of dark brown emulsion paint and a little white or cream.

5. Roughly stipple on the paint, using the dark and light colours as you did for the urn at Step 3.

6. If the corbel is to be displayed outside, it is best to seal it with two coats of exterior varnish to protect it from the weather, applying the second coat only after the first has dried. Alternatively, the paintwork may last very well as it is but will need retouching as it fades over time.

Two-hour transformations

As some of the projects in this section demonstrate, the secret is in learning to spot a bargain at a hundred paces and to recognize the potential in what the majority of people would dismiss as junk. You can then transform an ordinary item into something quite amazing!

Bamboo table and faux bamboo chair

Old bamboo furniture, covered in thick layers of paint that obliterate the bamboo can frequently be found in junk shops. It is well worth attempting to restore pieces like this table to their former glory, or stripping and repainting them sympathetically. The old chair frame has been given a bamboo-effect finish and reupholstered.

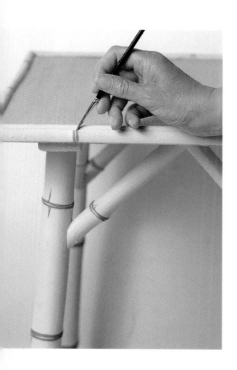

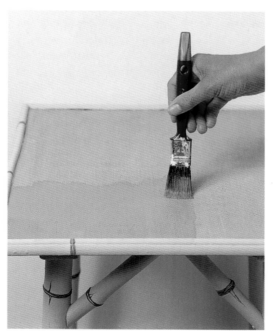

BAMBOO TABLE

You will need

Bamboo table, already stripped
Fine sandpaper
Beading and wood glue
Panel pins
Small hammer
White acrylic primer undercoat
1in (2.5cm) household paintbrushes
Matt emulsion paint in cream and fudge
No. 3 artist's paintbrush
Artist's acrylic tube paint in bamboo green (or use matt emulsion paint)
Shellac varnish and old paintbrush
Jam jar
Methylated spirits

Bamboo furniture is fashionable once again and in great demand. Besides original bamboo, there is a variety of authentic pieces in black or brown tortoiseshell finish, as well as lacquered and ebonized bamboo. There are many variations of faux bamboo finishes, too – some depicting the growth mark in the plant, the "eye", in terracotta, green or indigo. All are attractive, and it is a matter of taste in deciding which will look best in your home. A table such as this one is extremely versatile – being suitable as a side table anywhere in the house, as a plant table, with a lamp standing on it, or in a conservatory.

This table was stripped with paint stripper. The two tray

surfaces were in good condition, apart from the beading around the edges, which was renewed. The paint stripping was laborious and failed to remove all traces of colour from the crevices so the best option was to paint the table with a faux finish.

1. Make any necessary repairs to the table and sand any rough edges with fine sandpaper. Remove all of the dust and ensure the surface is clean before painting. If you need to attach new beading to the table, spread a little wood glue on the underside of the beading before positioning it in place and tapping in the panel pins.

2. Turn the table upside down and apply the first coat of white acrylic primer undercoat using a household paintbrush. (It will be easier to paint the table if it is stood on a table top or at working surface height.) If the paint feels difficult to spread, or shows too many thick brush-strokes, thin it with a little water. Turn the table upright and continue undercoating until all of the surfaces are covered. Brush away any paint drips and leave the paint to dry. Apply a second undercoat in the same way and leave to dry.

3. Paint the table all over with the cream emulsion as you did with the undercoat, ensuring that you always work along the length of the bamboo and in the same

direction as any grain or weave on the table top or tray. Leave the paint to dry.

4. Next, paint the tray surfaces of the table with the fudge-coloured emulsion, again working in the same direction as the weave or grain. Let the paint dry.

5. For a professional finish, apply a second coat of cream emulsion to the table frame and legs. Take care when painting the beading not to stray on to the darker top.

6. Using a no. 3 artist's paint-brush, paint circles of green paint over the growth lines on the bamboo and create false ones at intervals on the wooden beading. Accentuate the circles with small vertical marks.

7. If you think it necessary, very carefully apply another coat of fudge-coloured emulsion paint to the table top to finish it.

8. To complete the table and give it an antique look, pour some of the shellac varnish – which is spirit-based and dries quickly – into a small jam jar and replace the top. Brush on one coat of the shellac reasonably quickly and evenly, trying not to go back over previous brushstrokes since overbrushing will double the colour density and leave a dark patch which will spoil the final appearance. If the shellac seems difficult to apply, dilute it with a very little methylated spirits.

FAUX BAMBOO CHAIR

You will need

Old chair, already stripped
Shellac varnish and old
*   paintbrush*
White acrylic primer undercoat
1in (2.5cm) household
*   paintbrushes*
Matt emulsion paint in cream
Fine sandpaper
Artist's acrylic tube paint in
*   Hooker's green*
No. 3 artist's paintbrush
Artist's oil tube paint in
*   raw umber*
Jam jar with lid
White spirit
Old spoon
Fitch
Kitchen paper
Good-quality semi-matt
*   oil-based furniture varnish*
*   or polyurethane lacquer*

Old chair frames can be purchased for next to nothing. If the frame has been stripped or dipped, worm holes need not put you off – no worm will survive caustic! If it has been stripped by hand, or the worm looks active by tell-tale sawdust around the holes, buy some proprietary woodworm treatment and, working outside in the open, apply it to the wood. Carry out any repairs at this stage; for instance, if the joints are loose, squeeze in some wood glue. Clamp them, or pile up heavy books or weights on the chair and leave overnight.

You may have a suitable remnant in your own fabric collection; at worst you will have to buy 1yd (1m). The upholstery will probably cost about eight times more than the chair frame, but the finished piece will not only cost less than anything you could buy, but it will be absolutely unique and in the colours of your choice!

The chair pictured here is painted in a lovely old warm cream, which was sanded through on the edges for a more worn look and antiqued using raw umber oil tube paint mixed with white spirit. Dark green paint was used to highlight the back to suggest bamboo and to tone with the gingham checked fabric used to cover the newly upholstered seat. The chair should be upholstered only after the painted frame is finished.

If your chair frame is made of pine, elm or beech and appears pale or the colour of stripped pine, it will be possible to go ahead and simply apply the first coat of acrylic primer undercoat. However, if the frame is dark, it might be dark wood but more than likely it has been stained. If this is the case, even though stripped, the stain remains in the wood and shellac varnish is needed to create a barrier, preventing any stain left in the wood from "bleeding" into the paint and causing an unsightly stain, which would otherwise happen no matter how many coats of paint are applied.

1. If you need to create a barrier between dark woodstain and the paint, apply two coats of shellac varnish. Let the first coat dry before applying the second.

2. Turn the chair upside down and apply a first coat of white acrylic primer undercoat, using a household paintbrush. Turn the chair upright to finish the undercoat. Leave the paint to dry, before applying a second coat all over the chair in the same way.

3. Next, give the chair two coats of cream emulsion paint all over.

4. Using fine sandpaper, sand the squared edges on the chair back, down the sides and on the top where an old chair would logically be most worn.

5. Thin the Hooker's green acrylic tube paint with a little water and use it to paint the circular mouldings on the chair back, using a no. 3 artist's paintbrush. If the spindles are straight on your chair back and you do not have mouldings, paint instead faux bamboo circles and the little "eyes", or "V" marks, as you did on the bamboo table. Leave the paint to dry.

6. The next step is to antique the chair. Squeeze about 1in (2.5cm) of raw umber oil tube paint on to the lid of a jam jar. Add a little white spirit and mash the paint into the white spirit with a small brush, mixing well. Scrape the contents of the lid into the jar, and add about two tablespoons of white spirit.

7. Paint the antiquing liquid on to the chair using a fitch – starting at the back or one side of the chair until you feel confident, and the colour is right. Too dark a colour will obliterate the cream, while too light will not have much effect. Do not worry when the dirty liquid runs everywhere – you have not ruined it! Leave the liquid on for about 5 minutes – less in hot weather.

8. Remove the antiquing liquid from the top surfaces first using plenty of kitchen paper, allowing the liquid to remain in the little crevices and indentations to imitate the effects of where dust and dirt would have gathered over the years. How much of the antiquing liquid you remove is a matter of taste. You can wipe all of it off the top surfaces until the paper is clean if liked – the liquid will already have knocked back the colour, making it appear softer and older. (Should you have a disaster and not have noticed runs which have dried dark and streaky for instance, use neat white spirit to remove.)

9. It is important to leave the chair overnight to dry, and not to handle it at all in the meantime as any fingermarks will show.

10. To finish the chair, seal the paintwork with two coats of a good-quality semi-matt oil-based furniture varnish or polyurethane lacquer, allowing the first coat to dry thoroughly before applying the second. Finally, upholster the chair seat in a pretty fabric.

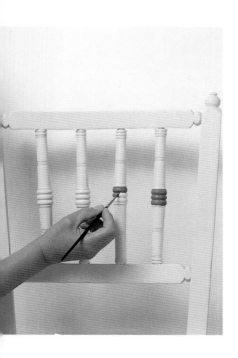

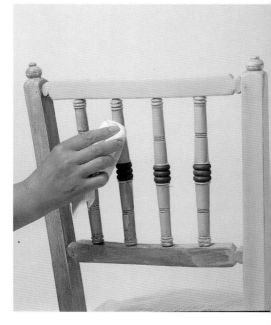

Tripod lamp

Originally, a tall ugly lacquered lamp stand, this piece was ideal for a transformation with metallic wax, and its wooden beads cried out to be treated like gemstones and provided the initial inspiration for this project. A brand new lampshade, painted in blue, white and pewter to match, completed the look.

LAMP STAND

You will need

Metal lamp stand

White polish or shellac varnish and old paintbrush

Matt emulsion paint in black (or use artist's acrylic tube paint in black or Payne's grey) and bright blue

Small brushes or fitches

Liberon gilt cream (Sceaux and St Germain)

Soft cloth

White acrylic primer undercoat, or matt or silk emulsion paint in white

Artist's acrylic tube paint in ultramarine blue and white

Jam jar lid

No. 8 artist's paintbrush

Unfashionable modern light fittings made from brassy metal with a shiny lacquered appearance, turn up at every auction sale in all shapes and sizes – often as part of a "lot" in a boxful of miscellaneous junk. Whether they are side lights or centrally fitted ceiling lights with three or four candle fittings covered by ugly glass shades, it is the sheer "brassiness" that is off-putting. The fact that they are metal, however, opens up a whole new area of possibilities.

There is a huge range of products on the market which have been formulated to enable the amateur to reproduce similar lookalike finishes of every kind, including metallic. These were previously available only to the few who could afford the services of an expert with highly

specialised skills. The new imitations cannot be compared with the real thing – gold paints, powders and waxes will never have the reflective brilliance, depth or beauty of gold leaf and real gilding, but we can now achieve the *effect*.

Metallic waxes are ideal in this instance. They are quick and easy to use and can be brushed on densely, as on the lamp base, or rubbed sparingly over colour for highlighting areas.

Your lamp stand will probably not require a coat of metal primer since this type of metal is usually rustproof. However, the paint is a precaution and does provide a "key" on which to paint since metal is slippery and is a difficult surface on which to paint directly. Alternatively, as long as the piece shows no signs of rust, a quicker and less messy option is to paint it, as here, with white polish which will also provide a good "key".

1. Clean the metal thoroughly, removing any dirt, grease or dust. Using an old brush, apply a coat of white polish or shellac varnish to the whole lamp stand, including the wooden roundels. Since white polish and shellac varnish are both fairly thin liquids, watch out for runs and drips. Leave to dry.

2. Leaving the wooden roundels untouched for now and working only on the metal, apply a coat of black emulsion or tube paint to the lamp stand. If using the latter, have a very little water on the brush and apply it almost neat from the tube. Leave the paint to dry, before applying a second coat of black to ensure a dense all-over covering.

3. Once the paint is dry, brush on the Sceaux gilt cream for the base metallic colour, using a fitch. Brush along the metal, in the same direction as any reeded or ridged design. Leave it until dry to the touch.

4. Again using a fitch, apply a little St Germain gilt cream to the raised surfaces to highlight them.

Leave to dry and set, before buffing the lamp stand to a shine with a soft cloth. Alternatively, you can leave it unpolished, as was done here.

5. Using a fitch, paint the wooden roundels white with the acrylic primer undercoat or emulsion paint, and apply a second coat when dry, if necessary. (The white makes an ideal base for allowing the vibrant bright blue paint to glow.)

6. When the white paint is dry apply two coats of bright blue emulsion paint to the roundels and let the paint dry.

7. Squeeze out about a 1in (2.5cm) line of both ultramarine blue and white acrylic tube paint on to a jar lid or other "palette". Using a no. 8 artist's paintbrush that has been dipped in water, pick up the blue paint on the brush. Begin by painting a wavy line diagonally across the first roundel from top to bottom on top of the blue base coat. Without cleaning the brush, dip it into the blue again and then the white and paint a few more wavy lines, twisting the brush as you work around the roundel (see the design on the lampshade). Continue all the way round, always keeping the blue paint

slightly wet, so that the white "waves" blend slightly, rather like the veins in marbling.

8. When you are satisfied with the effect, paint the other one or two roundels in the same way then leave to dry.

9. To finish the roundels give them a coat of white polish to protect them.

LAMPSHADE

You will need

Ruler
Pencil
Lampshade
Fitches or small paintbrushes
Decorator's acrylic varnish
*Matt emulsion paint in
    bright blue*
*Artist's acrylic tube paint in
    ultramarine blue, white
    and pewter*
Jam jar lids
No. 8 artist's paintbrush
Lining brush (optional)

The lampshade must be sufficiently deep, as well as wide, to look balanced on this tall, thin tripod lamp stand. The shade used here is made from natural fibres. Because the handmade paper is porous, the area of the shade to be painted is given two coats of decorator's acrylic varnish in order to stop the paint seeping into the paper.

1. Measure, and mark out in pencil around the bottom of the lampshade, a wide band of about 4–6in (10–15cm) deep – its width and position will depend on the size of the shade.

2. Using a fitch or a small brush, paint on two coats of decorator's acrylic varnish within the pencilled lines, allowing the first coat of varnish to dry before applying the second.

3. Next, apply the bright blue emulsion paint within the band, using a fitch or small brush, taking great care not to stray

over the pencilled lines. Allow the blue paint to dry, before applying a second coat.

4. Using the same technique as for the roundels on the lamp stand (see Step 7, page 34), squeeze out a little ultramarine blue and a little white acrylic tube paint on to a jar lid or similar "palette". Dip the no. 8 artist's paintbrush in water, then take up blue and white paint and twist it as you paint wavy lines on the blue band, making the paintwork look a little like the veins in marbling. Continue around the lampshade until it is

completed, replenishing the paint as you work.

5. Finally, to complete the painted design, squeeze a little pewter artist's acrylic tube paint on to a clean jar lid. Wet the artist's paintbrush or use a lining brush and draw it through the paint, making sure that the paint covers the brush evenly. Draw the brush along the pencilled lines to paint the pewter edging on the blue band. The pewter will cover any blue paint that has strayed over the edge of the band and gives your handiwork a professional finish.

Acanthus planter

The large spiny acanthus leaf has been depicted in architecture and interior decoration throughout the centuries. This acanthus planter, originally a humble mass-produced terracotta trough from Italy, looks extremely attractive with its bronze finish echoed by the deep chocolate and bronze tones of the plants within it.

You will need

Terracotta planter

Shellac varnish or white polish and old paintbrush

Matt emulsion paint in dark brown

1in (2.5cm) household paintbrush

Acrylic bronze metallic paint

Small paintbrush

Small fitch

Black patinating wax

Soft cloth

The acanthus leaf appears in many stately period homes and grand houses and has been painted on many different surfaces throughout the ages. It is also evident in plaster, carved in wood and in stone and woven into tapestries and carpets. The leaf was used in decorative scroll work in the late 18th century and also appeared on wallpaper introduced during this period.

Today acanthus scrollwork is often used for hand-painting antique furniture and classic panels, mirror frames and dadoes.

1. Check that the surface of the terracotta planter is dust-free and clean. Using an old brush, apply a coat of shellac varnish or white polish to seal the terracotta. Let it dry and apply a second coat if it looks patchy.

2. Paint the planter with the dark brown emulsion paint and leave to dry. Apply a second coat of paint if it seems necessary and leave to dry.

3. Apply a coat of the acrylic bronze metallic paint, using a small brush and stippling it on so as to avoid leaving any brush marks. Let it dry well.

4. Finally, use a fitch to apply the black patinating wax. Stipple the wax into areas on the planter that would be naturally darker than others, to add more texture and interest to the surface. Let the wax set and dry, before rubbing it from the raised surfaces using a soft cloth. Add more patinating wax if a darker effect is required.

Two cherubs

Cherubs have retained their popularity in interior decoration throughout the ages and while some look very ecclesiastical, others look like fat babies! Of the two cherubs here, the gilded seated cherub is handmade from reconstituted stone while the one on the wall is made in plaster and burnished with gold-coloured metallic wax.

BURNISHED GOLD CHERUB

You will need

Old spoon
Matt emulsion paint in blue-grey
Small plastic carton
Fitch
Plaster cherub
Kitchen paper
Small bristle brush

Shellac varnish diluted 1:1 with methylated spirits
Liberon gilt cream (Versailles)
Soft cloth

Cherubs appear in the architecture and interior decoration of many fine historical buildings, and were particularly favoured in baroque interiors,

often forming part of wonderful sconces or friezes, or as the centrepiece of decorative panels. Even in more modern times, cherubs are still popular and have recently enjoyed a revival, appearing on fabrics, wallpapers, lampshades, greetings cards and wrapping paper. You can often see them used in print form for decoupage decoration on walls

and decorative objects and as stencils with which to embellish walls and create borders.

Cherubic figures are made in several different media, including plaster, wood, resin, stone and even in plastic. The cherub above is made of plaster and has a flat back which means it is suitable only for displaying on a wall.

New bare plaster needs to be

wet in order to prime the surface. It can be brushed with water or "flooded" several times; it is amazing how quickly the water is absorbed.

1. Spoon some of the blue-grey emulsion paint or any coloured emulsion of your choice into a plastic carton and thin the paint with a little water.

2. Using a fitch, brush the plaster cherub with water all over once or twice. When the water has been absorbed, "flood" the plaster cherub with the watery blue-grey emulsion. Once the paint has been absorbed apply another coat. If the colour does not appear dense enough, add a little more paint to the liquid.

3. While the paint is still wet, gently rub it off some of the uppermost surfaces using kitchen paper, so as to give the cherub a worn appearance.

4. While the plaster is still damp, use a small bristle brush to apply the diluted shellac varnish, stippling it all over the cherub and into all the awkward areas – avoid using brushstrokes, which would show up later and spoil the effect. Since shellac varnish is partly soluble in water a porous surface such as this plaster, which has been wet or damp, will absorb the shellac to produce an attractive soft matt finish.

5. Leave the shellac varnish to dry for 10–15 minutes.

6. Apply the gilt cream to those uppermost surfaces of the cherub that you want highlighted with gold, using a brush or rubbing it on with kitchen paper. Leave for a few minutes before buffing the gilt cream with a soft cloth.

GILDED CHERUB

You will need

Stone cherub
Small paintbrushes
Matt or silk emulsion paint in turquoise
Acrylic gold size and small brush

Book of gold transfer leaf
Soft brush
Spirit-based lacquer in mid-oak, or white polish, or shellac varnish diluted 1:1 with methylated spirits, plus old paintbrush

This cherub, in a seated position, was originally inspired by a Carpeaux-sculpted frieze created in the 19th century for the Paris Opera House. Although it is the more accepted practice to use terracotta under gold leaf, the lovely greyish turquoise colour used here seemed more unusual. This cherub has many little awkward "nooks and

crannies" and it is important that these areas are properly cleaned, painted and gilded.

1. Clean the stone cherub well to remove any dirt or dust. Using a small paintbrush, paint the cherub thoroughly with the turquoise emulsion, making sure you coat it well with paint and especially all the little awkward areas. Let it dry before applying a second coat of paint. Leave to dry.

2. Brush the gold size on to the painted cherub, again taking care to get it into all the awkward areas. Leave for at least 15 minutes, until the size is tacky.

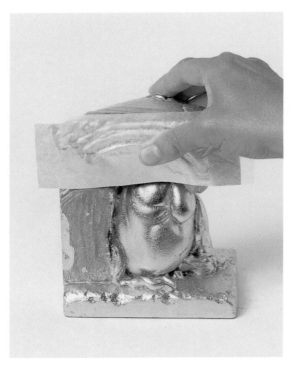

3. Take a sheet of gold transfer leaf and gently press it on to the gold-sized areas, smoothing your fingers over the sheet until all of the gold has transferred to the surface of the cherub. Remove the backing paper.

4. Very gently smooth down the gold leaf using a soft brush. You may have to stipple the leaf gently into the cherub's awkward "crevices" to make it adhere well to the gold size.

5. Continue in this way, carefully applying more sheets of gold leaf to the gold size until the surface of the cherub is covered with gold. There are bound to be small areas of background colour showing through, which is the whole idea, creating a look of slightly faded elegance.

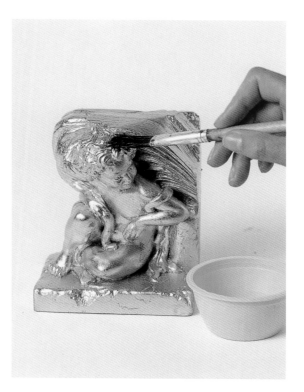
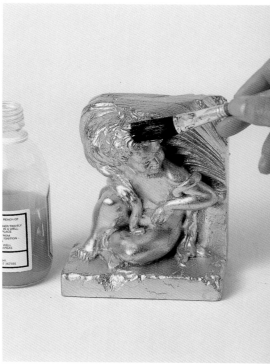

6. Leave the gilded surface to dry for 24 hours before proceeding to the next stage.

7. To complete the cherub paint it, as here, with a coat of "transparent" lacquer in a mid-oak colour for an antique effect. Alternatively, apply a protective coating of white polish to the gilded cherub or a coat of shellac diluted with methylated spirits.

TERRACOTTA PLASTER CHERUB

Another option using a plaster cherub is to paint it in a rich terracotta-coloured matt emulsion paint, as for Steps 1–3 of the Burnished Gold Cherub (see page 38).

When the plaster has completely dried out apply acrylic gold size all over using a small brush. Leave for at least 15 minutes, until tacky, before laying on gold leaf, following the instructions in Steps 3–4 of the Gilded Cherub.

Wearing a dust mask so as to avoid breathing in the fine powder, stipple on gold or bronze powder to fill any little inaccessible areas, Apply a sealing coat of white polish or shellac varnish diluted with methylated spirits to finish.

Pot pourri holders

Pot pourri is always popular and these pots and little Indian carved boxes make ideal alternatives to the usual array of pot pourri holders. They are also perfect for displaying the effects of the amazingly convincing metallic waxes now available.

WOODEN ROUND BOX WITH LID

You will need

Carved wooden round box
Shellac varnish and old paintbrush
Small bristle brush or fitch
Liberon gilt cream (Rambouillet and Sceaux)
Soft cloth

The three projects detailed here illustrate just some of the many different effects possible with emulsion paint and gilt cream. The basic method is the same in every case: wooden items are sealed first with shellac varnish in order to create a barrier between the woodstain and the paint or gilt cream to be used. Matt emulsion paint is then applied, if liked, gilt cream is brushed on top and a final polish with a cloth gives the shiny metallic look.

1. Ensure the wooden box is dust-free and paint the box and its lid with one coat of shellac varnish, applying it with an old brush. Let it dry.

2. Using a bristle brush or fitch, apply the Rambouillet gilt cream to the lid and all around the inside and outside of the box, always working the brush in one direction only. Leave to dry.

3. Highlight areas of the lid by brushing on the lighter-coloured Sceaux gilt cream, if liked. When dry, buff with a cloth to a shine.

PURPLE POT WITH HANDLE

You will need

Plastic pot
Small paintbrush
Matt emulsion paint in purple
Small bristle brush or fitch
Liberon gilt cream (St Germain)
Soft cloth

1. Ensure the pot is clean and dry. Using a small paintbrush, paint it all over, inside and out, with the purple emulsion paint and leave it to dry. Apply a second coat, making sure the pot

has a dense all-over covering of paint. Let the paint dry.

2. Using a bristle brush or fitch, apply the gilt cream to the pot, highlighting any raised surfaces such as the tops of ridges or fluting. Leave to dry, then buff the pot to a good metallic shine using a soft cloth.

CARVED WOODEN SQUARE BOX

You will need

Carved wooden square box (see opposite)
Shellac varnish and old brush
Small paintbrush
Matt emulsion paint in jade green
Small bristle brush or fitch
Liberon gilt cream (Versailles and Rambouillet)
Soft cloth

1. Ensure the box is dust-free and seal it inside and out with a coat of shellac varnish, using an old brush. Leave to dry.

2. Using a small paintbrush, paint the box all over with jade green emulsion, pushing your brush into the holes in the carved surfaces. Leave the paint to dry.

3. Using a bristle brush or fitch, apply the Versailles gilt cream by stippling it sparingly on to the box, avoiding the holes in the carved surfaces so as to leave these showing green. Let the gilt cream dry.

4. Buff the surfaces with a soft cloth, removing the colour slightly from the edges of the box, before highlighting these areas with a little Rambouillet gilt cream. Leave the gilt cream to dry before using a soft cloth to polish the surface to a good shine.

Morning makeovers

You will find here an interesting variety of inspirational projects to create in a morning. The cupboard will have to be prepared beforehand, and the tray, which is a quick and easy project, will have to be allotted a few minutes over the next two days if you want to craquelure it, but is well worth the little extra effort. The richly vibrant silk cushions will need a morning to complete each one, unless you are an absolute whizz at sewing!

French cupboard

An old cupboard, stripped to reveal an attractive pale oak frame and legs, was given this French-style look by the simple addition of a new shaped back at the top and a moulding, together with cleverly applied paintwork in café au lait colours. The cupboard was then antiqued to complete the effect.

You will need

Small cupboard, already stripped, sanded and prepared for painting

Shellac varnish and old paintbrush

Matt emulsion paint in fudge, cream and white (optional)

1in (2.5cm) household paintbrushes

Rule or straight edge

White chalk

Artist's paintbrushes

Moulding and wood glue (optional)

Tracing or greaseproof paper

Pencil

Black felt-tip pen

Low-contact masking tape

Lining brush

Artist's acrylic tube paint in raw umber and white (optional)

Carton lid or other "palette"

Kitchen paper

White acrylic primer undercoat

Vinyl silk/soft sheen emulsion paint in white, or decorator's acrylic varnish

Artist's oil tube paint in raw umber

Jam jar with lid

White spirit

Old spoon

Good-quality clear beeswax furniture polish

Soft cloth

Good-quality semi-matt oil-based furniture varnish or polyurethane lacquer

00 grade flour paper or fine cabinet paper

Paint stripper was used to remove dark, treacly varnish and stain from this little oak cupboard purchased at auction. It was then neutralized and sanded with an electric power sander to remove the remaining stain that had penetrated the grain in the wood. This revealed a lovely pale oak frame and legs, with ply panels on the sides and door. The unusual colour of the wood was the shade of old, faded French walnut and the cupboard had a French feel to it. By the time a new curved back and moulding had been added, it became the "French cupboard".

Since the wood could not be matched it was decided to paint the new shaped back the same colour as the ply panels. The colour of the wood had the greatest influence on the decision to adopt a two-tone theme of colours similar to those of natural linen and lace. These café au lait colours influenced the choice of simple scrollwork rather than a floral decoration. The simple trompe l'oeil shading added another dimension, as did the carved moulding on the back. The outside of the cupboard was antiqued and the inside painted white. Finally, the oak frame was enriched with wax polish to give a lustrous silk patina. However, the cupboard looked equally lovely, and the scrollwork was

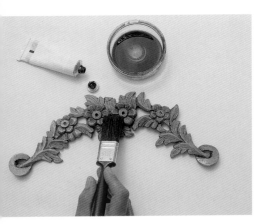

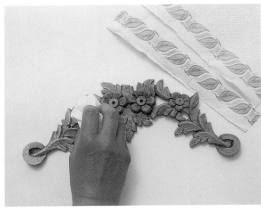

more sharply defined, before it was antiqued. If you prefer this look, omit the antiquing stage and instead varnish the piece or wax it two or three times directly over the emulsion paint, a day or two after it has dried.

1. Give the ply panels of your stripped cupboard two coats of shellac varnish, using an old brush, allowing the first coat to dry before applying the second. The shellac creates a necessary barrier, preventing any stain in the plywood from "bleeding" into the paint and causing an ugly stain, which would otherwise happen no matter how many coats of paint are applied on top.

2. When the shellac is dry, paint the ply panels and new back in the fudge-coloured emulsion, taking care not to stray on to the surrounding wood. They will require at least two coats of paint for good all-over cover. Let dry.

3. Depending on the size of your ply panels, decide on the width of the cream border required. Using a rule or straight edge as a guide, chalk a line around the inside of each panel to mark the border.

4. Using an artist's paintbrush, fill in the border with the cream emulsion paint (see picture, page 46), applying two or three coats for good cover. (Paint the moulding, if using, with cream emulsion paint now, too.) Allow the paint to dry.

5. Hold up the tracing or grease-proof paper against the door panel. Mark on the paper the outside edges and corners of the fudge-coloured panel with pencil to define its size. Remove the paper from the door and within this frame draw a narrow border and a simple scroll design, experimenting until you are satisfied with it. If the pencil marks are not clear enough, go over them with black felt-tip pen.

6. Turn the tracing paper over and go over the back of the lines showing through with the pencil. Turn the paper to the front once more and attach it to the door panel with masking tape. Repencil over the whole design to transpose the pencil markings on to the door panel (see picture, page 46). Do check from time to time that the design is showing up on the panel.

7. Remove the tracing paper and keep it for decorating the cupboard's side panels, although the design may need modifying. If you prefer, go over the pencil marks with chalk (see page 46).

8. Begin the painting with the narrow border for the trompe l'oeil effect of moulding for the inside edge of the cream "frame". The straight lines are achieved by using a lining brush, which is designed to maintain a thin flow of paint over a long line, since its hairs are longer than those in an artist's paintbrush. Squeeze a little raw umber acrylic tube paint on to the lid of a carton. With an artist's paintbrush, mix in a little water to a usable but not watery consistency. Wipe as much paint off this brush as possible to avoid wasting paint, then take up the lining brush and pull it through the raw umber paint until it is evenly covered.

9. Lay the cupboard on its back if possible. Position yourself comfortably and, steadying your little finger against the edge or on the surface, lay the lining brush on to the traced line on the inside edge of the cream "frame".

Begin to pull the brush towards you, laying all the hairs on to the surface almost up to the ferrule and watching the ferrule end of the brush as a guide while you paint. When the paint begins to run out, carefully lift off the brush and replenish it with paint. Overlap the line of paint a little when you replace the lining brush on the surface, and once again pull the brush towards you with a steady hand, ending at the very point of the corner of the panel. Move around the cupboard each time before painting the subsequent sides to complete the frame. Do not worry if you make a mess – simply keep a piece of damp kitchen paper handy to wipe away mistakes; then dry the surface and begin again.

10. Paint a second framing line in raw umber inside this one in the same way to create the three-dimensional moulding look. Since the left-hand side of the cupboard's front panel is darker (see main picture), shade between these two lines with raw umber, thinning the paint a little. Highlight the right-hand side of the cupboard's "moulding" with thinned cream emulsion paint.

11. Carefully fill in the area between the border and scroll-work with thinned white or cream emulsion or white acrylic tube paint.

12. Finally, paint the scroll design in cream emulsion, over-painting a second or third time until the cream stands out well against the background colour. Once dry, highlight with raw umber as before, to give a three-dimensional effect: paint raw umber on the outside edge of the scrolls on the left-hand side (see picture, page 46) and on the top edge of the scrolls at the bottom of the panel. Use a little raw umber on the inside edge of the scrolls on the lighter, right-hand side of the panel.

13. Once you are satisfied with the door panel, complete the cupboard's side panels following the same steps.

14. While the paint on the outside is drying, paint the inside of the cupboard in white primer undercoat. Let it dry then apply a second coat of either undercoat or matt emulsion in white. Finally, apply a top coat of white vinyl silk/soft sheen emulsion or a coat of decorator's acrylic varnish to protect the white paint. Leave to dry before applying a second top coat if necessary.

15. Once the cupboard is completely dry, the next step is to antique the outside. Squeeze

about 1in (2.5cm) of raw umber oil tube paint on to the lid of a jam jar. Add a little white spirit and mash the umber into it with a small brush. Scrape the contents of the lid into the jar, cleaning it off with the brush. Add two or three tablespoons of white spirit to the jar, stir well.

16. Begin on a side panel until you are confident enough to work on the front. Starting at the top, paint on the antiquing liquid in the same direction as the grain. Try to avoid letting the liquid run on to the unpainted wood by stemming the flow with kitchen paper. Leave for 5 minutes or until it begins to dry, then start removing the liquid with plenty of kitchen paper. Wipe the liquid off the paler areas first and work until the paper is almost clean. The liquid will already have knocked back the "newness", making the colour softer and older in appearance, although still remaining in the nooks and crannies where dust and dirt would be likely to have gathered over the years.

17. Antique the remaining panels and the moulding in the same way (see pictures opposite), removing the antiquing liquid from the top surfaces of the moulding with kitchen paper. Leave both the cupboard and the moulding overnight to dry out completely, without handling, since any fingermarks will show.

18. Glue the moulding to the cupboard (see picture opposite), following the manufacturer's instructions. Place the cupboard on its back if possible, or clamp the moulding in place overnight while the glue dries.

19. To finish the three panels, apply a generous coat of clear beeswax furniture polish to them and leave for 10–15 minutes, before polishing with a soft cloth. Alternatively, apply a coat of oil-based varnish or polyurethane lacquer to the panels to protect them and leave to dry overnight.

Leave the panels varnished only or, two days later, when the varnish has completely dried, apply clear beeswax polish on top.

20. To complete the cupboard, apply a coat of good-quality clear beeswax furniture polish to the bare wood to give it a rich, silk-like patina. Leave to dry for 10–15 minutes. Take a sheet of fine flour or cabinet paper and sand the wax into the wood, working in the same direction as the grain. Reapply the wax, then leave it to dry before polishing with a soft cloth.

Cream candlestick lamp

The overall colour scheme gives this lamp a sense of faded elegance that would fit into any antique setting. The base has been painted in a buttermilk shade and antique gold before being given a craquelure finish, and the thin card lampshade has been transformed by a beautiful antique Maltese lace collar.

You will need

Medium Density Fibreboard (MDF) or turned softwood candlestick lamp base

White acrylic primer undercoat

1in (2.5cm) household paintbrushes

Fine sandpaper

Matt emulsion paint in cream

Jam jars with lid

Artist's acrylic tube paint in raw umber and gold

No. 4 or 5 artist's paintbrush

Kitchen paper

Two-part craquelure kit (see page 11)

Washing-up liquid

Hair dryer

Artist's oil tube paint in raw umber

White spirit

Good-quality semi-matt oil-based varnish or polyurethane lacquer

Card lampshade in cream

Lace

Fabric glue

Low-contact masking tape

The lamp base shown here is a candlestick shape, made from MDF and available through mail order. It has been painted in cream emulsion and the mouldings painted in antique gold – the colour mixed using artist's acrylic tube paints. A craquelure finish gives the lamp character, and was followed by an application of antiquing liquid to age it and varnish to seal it.

Good-quality card lampshades with a parchment appearance, like the one used here, are widely available. The lace has been draped around it and glued on to the shade.

1. Keeping the electric flex out of the way, apply a coat of white acrylic primer undercoat to the lamp base, using a household paintbrush. Let it dry.

2. When the paint has dried the MDF surface will probably feel a little rough after the application

of paint. If this is the case, sand the lamp base carefully with fine sandpaper, paying special attention to the mouldings until they feel smooth to the touch.

3. Apply a second coat of primer undercoat to the lamp base and leave the paint to dry.

4. Paint the primed lamp base with two coats of cream emulsion, letting the first coat dry before applying the second.

5. Pour some water into a jam jar. Squeeze a little raw umber acrylic tube paint and the same amount of gold paint on to the jar lid or a similar "palette". Using an artist's paintbrush, mix some, not all, of the two colours

together with a little water. You will soon find the right consistency of paint with which it is best to work.

6. Brush the antique gold-coloured paint on to the lamp base mouldings, using a no. 4 or no. 5 artist's paintbrush. Use more of the raw umber paint on the first coat, gradually adding more gold until the colour is to your liking. Work around each moulding in the same direction. You will probably need to give the mouldings three coats of the paint in order to cover the brush-strokes and give a smooth finish. Leave each coat to dry – about 10 minutes – before applying the next one. Have a piece of kitchen paper handy for speedily wiping

away any stray gold paint. Leave the mouldings to dry.

7. Now begin the craquelure process. Using a clean brush, paint the ageing varnish sparingly on to the cream paint of the lamp base. Brush on the varnish evenly and watch out for drips. Leave the varnish to dry for at least 6 hours, by which stage it will feel barely tacky, or better still leave it overnight by which time it will feel dry. The drier the tack of the varnish, the smaller the cracks will be.

8. Next, apply the water-based crackle varnish sparingly, using a brush. You will notice a lot of air bubbles and brush marks appear. To get rid of these put the brush

down and gently massage the surface with your fingers. This helps the varnish to adhere well before it dries and counteracts bubbles and brush marks. Hold the lamp base up to an oblique light which reflects on the surface; if you can still see brush marks or "holes", dip a fingertip into a drop of washing-up liquid, and massage it into the varnish before it dries. This should solve the problem. Leave for at least 1 hour or, better still, overnight.

9. The next step is to apply a little warmth to the varnished surface, using a hairdryer. With the hairdryer switched to warm – not hot which would blister the varnish – gently blow it over the surface. Work carefully and patiently and eventually you will see minute fissures appearing over the surface of the varnish.

10. To antique the craquelure, mix some raw umber oil tube paint in a jar with a little white spirit. Rub the paint evenly into the cracked varnished surface using a small paintbrush or kitchen paper.

11. Once the surface is covered with the paint, wipe off the excess with kitchen paper working in a circular motion and pushing the raw umber into the cracks. Continue wiping the surface of the lamp base until the kitchen paper is almost clean, leaving the colour only in the cracks in the varnish. Leave overnight to dry.

12. Because the crackle varnish is water soluble the craquelure surface must now be sealed with a coat of an oil-based varnish. This will also take away the unattractive shine once the crackle varnish is dry.

13. Complete the lamp by covering a suitable card lamp-shade with antique lace. Use fabric that has a pretty scalloped edge, deep enough to cover the lampshade, and attach it to the inside of the shade at the very top, using any glue suitable for fabric. Hold the lace in place with low-contact masking tape until the glue has dried and the tape can be removed.

Jewellery box & hand mirror

A shabby old box has been treated to a finish of deep purple paint over a simple inlaid design of silver leaf, and is teamed with a 1930s wooden hand mirror – given the same treatment but with the addition of a few decoupaged roses.

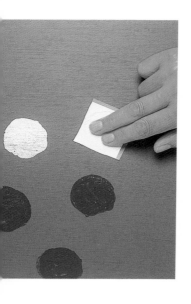   

JEWELLERY BOX

You will need

Wooden box
Shellac varnish and old paintbrush
Small paintbrushes
Matt emulsion paint in black or dark
    grey and deep purple
Jam jar
Ballpoint pen
Acrylic gold size and small brush
Book of aluminium and/or silver
    transfer leaf
Small soft brush
White polish

Old spoon
PVA glue
Plastic carton with lid
Artist's acrylic tube paint in
    Payne's grey
Lightweight gloves
Small natural sea sponge
Kitchen paper

1. Paint the box, inside and out, with shellac varnish using an old brush. Let the shellac dry. If the piece was dark-stained, apply a second coat of shellac and leave it untouched to dry.

2. Using a small paintbrush, paint the box with two coats of black or dark grey emulsion paint, allowing the first coat to dry before applying the second. Leave it to dry. Paint the inside of the box in the same way and prop the box lid open each time so that it does not stick.

3. In a jam jar or other suitable container, mix some of the deep purple emulsion paint with a small amount of black or dark grey to create the colour required. Apply two coats of this

colour to the box, allowing the first coat to dry before applying the second.

4. Using a ballpoint pen, mark out rough circles at random over the surface of the box and lid. They do not have to be exact since they are meant to represent pools of light and will be partially sponged over later.

5. Brush on the gold size within the ballpoint pen circles, a few at a time. Leave for at least 15 minutes, until the size is tacky.

6. Take a sheet of aluminium or silver leaf to lay on the first circle. (To use it economically, either cut the sheet into pieces or start in one corner of the sheet.) Lay the leaf, with the backing paper attached, directly on to the circle. Smooth it out with your fingers and remove the backing paper with the remaining leaf attached. Repeat the process with the other circles. Keep the leaf leftovers, however small – they will be useful for filling-in another time. Once the first group of circles has been covered in transfer leaf, remove the frayed edges carefully using a soft brush. Move on to the next area of circles and work until all are completed. Leave for 1–2 hours, until the gold size is dry. Paint the whole box with a coat of white polish to seal, then leave to dry.

7. Using an old spoon, measure out equal parts of purple emulsion paint and PVA glue into the base of a plastic carton.

Stirring well, mix them with up to four parts water to make up an emulsion glaze. Use the carton lid as a palette and squeeze on to it a small amount of Payne's grey acrylic tube paint.

8. Wearing lightweight gloves, squeeze out the natural sea sponge in clean water to soften it, then squeeze it a second time in kitchen paper to remove the excess water. Dip only part of the sponge into the glaze and begin sponging the surface of the box. You are aiming for a closely sponged finish, not the wide open sponge marks you might expect on a wall. Occasionally, dip the tip of the sponge into the Payne's grey tube paint, after replenishing the sponge first with the glaze. Carefully sponge between the silver circles and slightly over their edges.

9. Prop the box lid open to dry. If the surface paint coverage looks a bit thin, sponge over it again,

introducing a little Payne's grey as well as the deep purple direct from the tin – always dipping the sponge into the glaze first. (Wash the sponge out well in warm soapy water immediately afterwards, otherwise the PVA glue will make it rock hard.)

10. Once the surface is dry, open the lid to its fullest extent, in order to lay the transfer leaf around the edges of the box. Work out a simple scroll pattern for the outside top edge and the escutcheon. Draw directly on to the surface in ballpoint pen. Paint on the gold size inside and up to the ballpoint outline, being meticulously accurate – remember wherever there is gold size the leaf will adhere to it!

11. Cut the transfer leaf into long narrow strips and lay one on the gold-sized area. Smooth out as before. Peel back the backing paper when you are sure it is stuck down on the surface.

12. Remove the overlapping frayed edges using a soft brush, as before, then apply the next strip of transfer leaf, slightly overlapping the last one.

13. When all the newly decorated areas have completely dried, finish the box by applying a coat of white polish or shellac varnish to seal the silver and paint finish.

HAND MIRROR

You will need

Wooden hand mirror
Low-contact masking tape
Shellac varnish and old
    paintbrush
Matt emulsion paint in black or
    dark grey and deep purple
Small paintbrushes
Jam jar
Tracing or greaseproof paper
Pencil
Ballpoint pen

Acrylic gold size and small
    brush
Book of aluminium and/or silver
    transfer leaf
Small soft brush
White polish
Small sharp pointed scissors
1 sheet good-quality floral
    wrapping paper
Reusable adhesive
Chalk
Pasting board
Small pasting brush
Ready-mixed heavy-duty
    wallpaper paste
Craft knife
Kitchen paper
Small sponge
Tack cloth
Acrylic lacquer suitable for
    decoupage or good-quality
    oil-based furniture varnish

There are many delightful alternatives to the roses for the decoupage design on the back of the mirror: butterflies, birds, a single spray of flowers, even a favourite photograph which has been photocopied. The possibilities are endless.

1. First tape around the edge of the mirror with masking tape to protect the glass, then paint the mirror with shellac varnish and with emulsion paint following Steps 1–3 of the Jewellery Box (see page 54). It may be necessary to give the mirror a third coat of the darkened purple emulsion for a good all-over covering of paint.

2. Work out a pretty scroll design for the silver leaf for the back of your mirror. Sketch out a pattern on a piece of tracing paper in an oval or other shape, depending on the style of your mirror. Turn the tracing paper over and go over the back of the lines showing through with the pencil. Turn the paper to the front once more and place it on the mirror back. Repencil over the design to transpose the pencil markings on to the mirror. Repeat for the handle on the other side – the design could match that of the escutcheon on the box if liked – then go over all the lines with a ballpoint pen for an accurate fine outline.

3. Using a small brush, paint on the gold size inside and up to the ballpoint outline, being meticulously accurate as before – since wherever there is gold size the silver will adhere to it.

4. Cut out and apply the aluminium or silver leaf, following Steps 11 and 12 of the Jewellery Box.

5. When the gilded surface has dried out, seal it with a coat of white polish or shellac varnish and leave to dry.

6. For the decoupage, cut out from the floral wrapping paper about eight flower heads, an equal number of buds and some leaves, using pointed scissors (see page 84 for the cutting technique).

7. Arrange the cut-outs within the silver leaf scrollwork on the back of the mirror. Temporarily secure the cut-outs in place with reusable adhesive, removing it as you work. If you like, you could also lightly chalk around the edges of the cut-outs to mark their outline, which is helpful for replacing them in the correct position on the mirror once they have been pasted.

8. Select a cut-out and place it face down on your pasting board. Brush over the paste evenly, working from the centre outwards and over the edges. Lift the cut-out off the board, using a craft knife if it helps, and replace it on the mirror back within the chalk marks, if using. Move it into the exact position before pressing it flat from the centre outwards, to remove excess paste and air

bubbles. Press the edges down and clean up with damp kitchen paper. Continue in this way with the remaining cut-outs until the decoupage design is complete. When it is dry, clean up the surface of the paper using more kitchen paper or a damp sponge, taking care not to damage it.

9. Wipe the surface with a tack cloth before finishing the mirror by applying a coat of either acrylic lacquer suitable for decoupage or a good-quality oil-based furniture varnish. (Since the white polish is spirit based, it will tolerate either finish.) Complete with another one or two coats to protect the mirror from wear, checking, as always, the manufacturer's instructions for drying times.

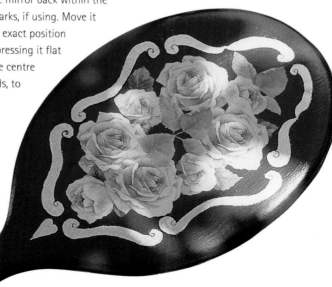

Exotic suliman silk cushions

These richly coloured silk cushions in oleander pink, granadilla purple, burnt orange and gold evoke the scents and colours of far horizons: jasmine and joss sticks, and spices such as saffron and cinnamon, chilli, cumin and ginger. Combine them with handwoven carpets in wondrous colours, antique sari braids and embroideries, and intricately carved pieces in wood and metal to continue the exotic theme.

FRILLED SQUARE CUSHION

You will need

8³⁄₄in (22cm) square of purple silk for the front square (optional), plus 4 strips 6in (15cm) by the width of the fabric (48 or 54in/ 122 or 137cm) for the frill
Tape measure
Iron
Pins, including a long glass- or bead-headed pin
Sewing machine
14¹⁄₂in (37cm) square of pink silk for the cushion cover front, plus 22¹⁄₂ x 14¹⁄₂in (57 x 37cm) rectangle for the back
Scissors
Matching thread and needle
13–14in (33–36cm) square cushion pad

These cushions demonstrate the sheer pleasure of the texture of silk, which appears "shot" as it reflects the light, emphasizing soft folds, frills and curves. There is a whole spectrum of Indian-style colours from which to choose, and each one will create an immediate impact in any room. Red is distinctive and dramatic, the colour of love, fire and passion, while purple is a truly regal shade. The vibrant oleander pink and the burnt orange used here look fabulous, but perhaps the gold used against these colours has the greatest impact. These stripes would never be used in an Indian design – this is purely an adaptation for a zingy effect!

One yard (1m) of silk will easily make two cushions and any leftover fabric can be used creatively to make contrasting frills and borders.

It is quite common for Indian cushions to have an overlapped opening in the back, as here, which is a very simple way of getting the cushion pad into the cover. However, a zip will give the cushion a tighter more "stuffed" appearance (as will a larger cushion pad) and look more professional. Another option is to hand sew (rather than machine stitch) one side of the cushion cover with the intention of carefully unpicking it when you need to dry-clean the cushion cover.

If you decide upon a zip, it is simpler to insert it in the back square of the cover (see the alternative instructions on the next page) rather than fighting with fraying silk, a frill and a zip all along the same edge.

1. Take the purple square, if you wish to have this in the centre of your cushion front, and turn under and press a ³⁄₄in (2cm) seam allowance along all four sides. Pin then machine stitch it in the centre of the pink square, right sides uppermost.

2. To make the overlapped opening in the back of the cushion cover, cut the rectangle of pink silk in half to make two pieces measuring 14¹⁄₂ x 11¹⁄₄in (37 x 28.5cm). Turn under 1in (2.5cm) on the two edges you have just cut and press then machine stitch.

3. With both wrong sides uppermost and the hemmed edges towards each other, lay one piece on top of the other to overlap by 6in (15cm). First pin the two pieces together, then machine stitch along both sides of the now square back cover to secure the overlap.

4. To make the frill for edging the cushion, pin then machine stitch the four purple strips together to form one long strip, always ensuring you stitch the right sides of the fabric together. Machine stitch the two ends together to make a continuous band, then press all the seams open. Fold the band in half, the wrong sides of the fabric together, and press.

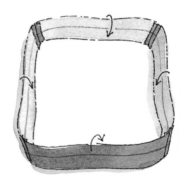

5. Cut an extra long length of thread to use doubled for strength for gathering the fabric. Start by securing the thread well at one "corner" of the band by oversewing a few stitches then sew the long edges of the band together, using a loose running stitch (see the similar frill made in Step 5 of the Long-Tailed Rosette, page 18).

6. Draw the fabric along the thread to gather it and make a continuous frill to fit the outside edges of the cushion. Secure the loose ends of thread temporarily by wrapping them in a figure of eight around a glass- or bead-headed pin stuck into the frill.

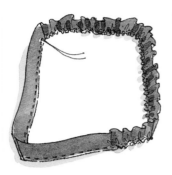

7. Pin the frill in place on to the right side of the cushion cover front. When you are satisfied with it, secure the bunched-up folds on each corner with a pin placed well away from the stitching line; otherwise it may snap your sewing machine needle. Check that the frill is evenly spread and tucked in towards the middle of the cushion cover. You will be able to adjust the gathers slightly as you machine stitch. (Alternatively, you could baste the frill on to the cover first, if preferred.)

8. With right sides together, place the cushion cover back on top of the frilled square and pin in position. Slowly and carefully, machine stitch ³⁄₄in (2cm) from

the edge through all the layers, removing the pins and readjusting the frill as you work. Keep checking that the fabric is not getting caught up underneath. Go over the seams with a second row of machine stitching once you are certain the stitches are in the right place.

9. Trim the frayed edges of the silk and turn the cushion cover the right side out. Insert the cushion pad, folding it in half first to make it easier.

USING ZIPPING FOR AN ALTERNATIVE OPENING

Having a zip in the back of the Frilled Square Cushion is an alternative to the overlapped opening. It requires less fabric for the cushion cover back than the overlapped opening (only

16¹⁄₂ x 14¹⁄₂in/42 x 37cm), and you will need zipping cut to 16in (40.5cm). Zipping is available by the yard or metre, or by the roll, from upholstery and fabric shops and can be opened either end.

These instructions for making a zipped cushion back and for inserting zipping may be applied to any cushion: although the measurements may differ, the principle is the same.

1. To make the cushion cover back, cut across the longest side of the rectangle of fabric to create two pieces, one measuring about 13in (33cm) deep and the other 3¹⁄₂in (9cm).

2. Turn under 1in (2.5cm) on the two edges you have just cut and press. Pin then baste a length of zipping between these two pressed edges, leaving one end of the zipping protruding by about

1½in (4cm). Machine stitch the zipping in place.

3. Open the protruding end of the zipping by about 1in (2.5cm) and cut a "V" shape down into the teeth so that the pointed ends of the fabric are longer. This gives something to hold on to while you slide the zip opener on to one line of "teeth". Push the teeth of the other side into the opener and slide the opener within the square of fabric by about 1in (2.5cm). Trim the zipping in line with the edge of the fabric and complete the cushion cover in the usual way.

GOLD AND PURPLE STRIPED CUSHION

You will need

22 x 3in (56 x 7.5cm) strip of purple silk for the stripe
22 x 3in (56 x 7.5cm) strip of gold silk for the stripe, plus two 20 x 6in (51 x 15cm) and two 16 x 6in (41 x 15cm) strips for the cushion border
Tape measure
Iron
18 x 14in (46 x 36cm) rectangle of pink silk for the cushion cover front, plus 18 x 16in (46 x 41cm) rectangle for the back
Pins
Sewing machine
Scissors
Matching thread and needle

Zipping cut to 20in (51cm)
16 x 12in (41 x 30.5cm)
cushion pad

1. Neaten the raw edges of the purple and gold stripes for the cushion cover front by turning under ¾in (2cm) along both long edges of the stripes and pressing.

2. With all right sides uppermost, place the two stripes diagonally across the narrower pink rectangle, leaving no gap in between them. Pin then sew the stripes in position to make the front cover, machine stitching close to the edges of the stripes.

3. Next, make the cushion cover back. Cut across the other pink rectangle lengthways to create two pieces, one 4in (10cm) deep and the other 12in (30.5cm). Turn under 1in (2.5cm) on the two edges you have just cut and press. Pin, baste and then machine stitch the zipping between these two edges, leaving one end of the zipping to protrude by about 2in (5cm), which will enable you to slide on the zip opener (see left).

4. Once the zipping is machine stitched in place, slide the zip opener within the fabric rectangle by about 1½in (4cm) and trim the zipping in line with the edge of the fabric.

5. Place together the wrong sides of the two pink rectangles –

which are now both the same size – so that the cushion looks as it will when finished. Baste the two pieces together.

6. Now have the cushion cover horizontally in front of you with the striped front cover uppermost. With right sides together, lay one of the longer strips of gold at the top edge of the cover, centering it across the width of the cover. Pin then machine stitch the two pieces together, again stitching 1in (2.5cm) from the edges.

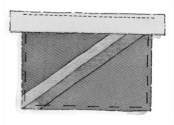

7. Lift the gold border you have just stitched and open it out. Attach the next strip of gold border in the same way.

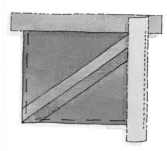

8. When all four strips have been attached to the striped front, fold back all the gold borders and lay them out flat.

9. To make the mitred corners, turn the cover over so that the zipped cushion cover back is uppermost. Turn up the excess fabric at each corner, which will form triangles. Pin the bases of these triangles of fabric together diagonally from the corners and machine stitch. Trim away the excess fabric.

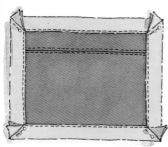

10. With the cushion back still uppermost, turn in the outer edge of the gold border by ¾in (2cm) all round and press. Then fold the border down, wrong sides together, so that the turned edge meets the seam line and press in place. At the corners press along the base of the triangles of excess fabric that will again form and stand up. This will help indicate the stitching line for the next step.

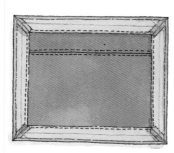

11. When it is well pressed, unfold the gold border and roughly flatten it out.

12. Working first from the top left-hand corner of the cushion, fold the gold border to meet at the corner, right sides together, bending the cushion fabric back on itself.

13. Pin then machine stitch along the pressed line which is roughly at right angles to the first mitred seam.

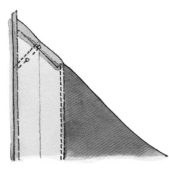

14. Trim the excess fabric, then move on to the other three corners, treating them in the same way.

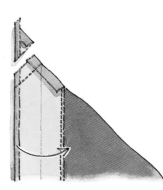

15. Turn the gold border the right side out and pin then slipstitch it in place to complete the cushion cover. Insert the cushion pad.

ROUND BUTTONED CUSHION

You will need

Scissors
18 x 16in (46 x 40.5cm)
rectangle of orange silk for
the cushion cover back,
plus 16in (40.5cm) square
for the front
Tape measure
Iron (set on silk setting)
Pins, including a long glass or
bead-headed pin
Matching thread and needle
Sewing machine
Zipping cut to 18in (46cm)
3 strips 5in (13cm) by the
width of the fabric (48 or
54in/122 or 137cm) of
purple silk for the frill, plus
a little extra to cover the
buttons
14in (36cm) round cushion pad
2 metal buttons with snap-on
black plates (for covering
with fabric)
Button cord and long needle
with a very large eye

1. To make the cushion cover back, cut across the longest side of the orange rectangle to create two pieces, one 6in (15.5cm) deep and the other 12in (30.5cm).

2. Turn under 1in (2.5cm) on the two edges you have just cut and press. Pin, baste and then machine stitch the zipping between these two edges, leaving one end of the zipping protruding by about 2in (5cm), which will enable you to slide on the zip opener (see page 60).

3. Slide the zip opener within what is now a square by about 1in (2.5cm). Cut a 16in (40.5cm) diameter circle out of each orange silk square.

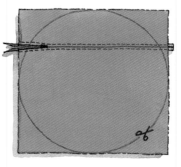

4. To make the frill, machine stitch all three purple strips together, always keeping the right sides together, to form one long strip. Press all the seams open. Fold the strip in half lengthways, wrong sides together, and press.

5. Proceed as you did for the Frilled Square Cushion (see Steps 5 and 6, page 60), starting by cutting an extra long length of thread to use doubled for strength for gathering the fabric. Secure the thread well at one end of the band by oversewing a few stitches then sew the long edges of the band together, using a loose running stitch.

6. Draw the fabric along the thread to gather the frill to a length to match the circumference of the cushion and allowing for an extra 3–4in (7.5–10cm) for the ends of the frill to overlap. Secure the loose ends of thread temporarily by wrapping them in a figure of eight around a glass- or bead-headed pin stuck into the frill.

7. Pin the frill in place on to the right side of the cushion cover front, making sure that one end of the frill overlaps the other and that both ends taper off the cushion cover front at an angle so that the raw edges will be within the inside of the cushion when it is turned the right side out. Check that all of the frill is evenly spread out and tucked in towards the middle. You will be able to adjust it slightly as you machine stitch.

Instead of using suliman silk for these cushions, other possibilities include using either dressmaking fabric in shot taffeta which comes in a wide range of rich colours that reflect the light, or dupion, which is a slub silk although the darker sea greens and blues also have a "shot" appearance.

Do take care when stitching silk or the fabric will pull and pucker. It helps to ensure accurate and plentiful pinning when working with silk, and basting pieces in position first is always a good idea. Be aware, too, that silk fabrics are particularly prone to fading in bright sunlight so do not leave silk cushions in front of bright windows day after day.

Another possible fabric is Indian cotton, woven with two vibrant colours is sometimes corded, which would lend itself well to these cushion.

Button forms for covering with fabric yourself are widely available and come in a range of sizes. Instead of using these, however, you could substitute fancy decorative buttons from good stores or haberdasheries.

Another idea for your cushions, if you do not want to make your own frill, is to attach to the cushion edges either tasselled fringing or a string of heavy lampshade bobbles, made especially for soft furnishings.

8. With right sides together, place the cushion cover back, with the zip partially open, on top of the frilled front piece. Pin the two circles in position and then baste them together.

9. Slowly and carefully, machine stitch around the circumference of the circles, 1in (2.5cm) from the edge of the fabric, stitching through all the layers and readjusting the frill as you work. Keep checking that the silk is not getting caught up underneath.

Go over the seams with a second row of machine stitching once you are certain the stitches are in the right place.

10. Trim the zipping and the frayed edges of the silk and turn the cushion cover the right side out. Insert the cushion pad and fasten the zip.

11. To give the cushion a truly professional finish cut out two small circles of purple silk for covering the buttons, slightly larger than the circumference of your buttons. Take a needle and thread and hand sew a loose running stitch around the edges of each circle of fabric. Place a button in the centre of each circle; carefully draw the thread to gather the fabric tightly around the button and fasten the thread securely. Snap on the back plate of each button to hold the fabric tight.

12. Tie a length of strong button cord (or other suitable unbreakable thick thread), through the loop of one button and make a firm knot. Thread the other end of the cord through a large-eyed needle. Pass it through the centre of the cushion cover and pad to meet the button loop on the other side. Slot through the second button loop and knot the cord as tightly as possible to finish your cushion.

Oval tray

The charming oval shape of this new plywood tray proved irresistible! Painted in a lovely old shade of grey-green with a simple hand-painted design of intertwined ribbons in sharp summery colours, the tray was then aged with a craquelure and antique finish. It is perfect for serving drinks, tea in the garden or breakfast in bed.

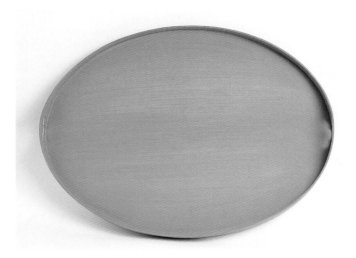

You will need

240 grade sandpaper
Oval plywood tray
White acrylic primer undercoat
1in (2.5cm) household paintbrushes
Matt emulsion paint in blue-grey and grey-green
Old spoon
Jam jars with lid
White chalk
Tape measure
Rule or straight edge
Artist's acrylic tube paint in pink, turquoise and green for the ribbons (or use matt emulsion paint), and in white, raw umber and gold
Plastic carton lid or other "palette"
Nos. 4 and 3 artist's paintbrushes

Kitchen paper
Lining brush
Two-part craquelure kit (see page 11)
Washing-up liquid
Hairdryer
Artist's oil tube paint in raw umber
White spirit
Good-quality semi-matt oil-based furniture varnish or polyurethane lacquer

Oval-shaped plywood trays like the one used here are available through mail order and similar trays in other shapes and sizes are possible, too.

1. Using the 240 grade sandpaper, sand any rough patches of plywood – usually to be found around the handles and on the edges of the tray. Remove the dust created.

2. Using a household paintbrush, give the tray a coat of acrylic primer undercoat, slightly thinned with water. Paint both sides of the tray, watching out for paint runs through the handle cut-outs so you can brush these away. Let the paint dry.

3. When the paint has dried the ply surface will feel a little rough after the application of paint. Using fine sandpaper again,

gently sand the large surfaces of the tray first and then the edges. Always use the sandpaper in the same direction as the grain in the wood, working until the surfaces feel smooth to the touch.

4. Apply a second coat of acrylic primer and leave it to dry.

5. Give the tray a coat of blue-grey emulsion for the base colour. Begin on the inside of the tray's sides then progress to the main part of the tray, neatening the brushstrokes as you work. Let the paint dry before turning the tray over and painting the other side. Once the paint is dry, apply a second coat all over as before.

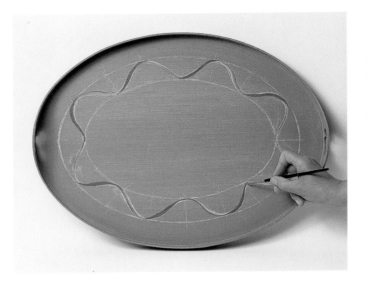

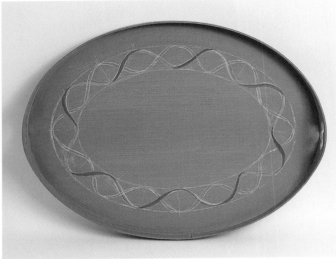

6. Measure a teaspoonful of the grey-green emulsion into a jam jar and thin it with a little water. Use this to brush over the base colour on the tray. Always keep the brushstrokes going in the same direction for a smart finish. Overbrush again until the paint-work looks good.

7. Make chalk marks at intervals, about 2in (5cm) in from the inside edge of the tray and use these as a guide by which to chalk a line all the way round. Chalk a second line 2in (5cm) inside the first to create a wide oval band.

8. Now make chalk marks on the inner line opposite the centre of the tray's sides and by the handles, to divide the band into quarters. Make more marks about 2in (5cm) apart in each quarter of the oval band. Even up the

distance between the marks if necessary. Using a rule, lengthen the marks into lines to divide the band into equal-sized sections. Finally, using the chalk marks as a guide, mark out the position of the first winding ribbon.

9. Place a little of the pink and turquoise colours on your carton lid palette. Whether using artist's acrylics or emulsion paint for the ribbons, you will need a little white acrylic tube paint on the palette, too, to achieve the shading, which helps to give the realistic twisted ribbon appearance.

10. Dip the no. 4 artist's paint-brush into the pink paint, wipe the brush on the side of the lid, to remove the paint from one side only, then dip the cleared side into the white paint to give you pink on one side and white

on the other, while the brush should look fairly flat. Taking advantage of the flattened shape of the tip of the brush, begin the brushstroke as if intending to paint a fine line. Now press down on the surface to open the brush out more, finally releasing the pressure and bringing the brush up to its tip again. These combined movements give the twisted ribbon effect. It will not be possible to continue this in one stroke – the ribbon has to be painted in sections. Remove the brush from the surface of the tray. Replenish the paint as before, flattening the brush by wiping it on the side of the palette and begin a new section in the same way. When the pink ribbon is complete leave the paint to dry.

11. Outline the second, intertwining ribbon in chalk –

running it under and over the pink ribbon – before painting it in turquoise in exactly the same way as the first ribbon.

12. Place a little green paint on your palette for the border lines. Rinse the lining brush in water then run it through your fingers to get a perfect "line" shape, before pulling it through the paint until it is loaded evenly – but not overloaded which will make a mess! Position yourself comfortably so as to be able to pull the lining brush towards you. Steady your little finger against the edge of the tray to ensure a good line, before laying the tip of the brush exactly on the line. Now, without pressing, lay all the hairs of the lining brush down and pull the brush towards you, watching its ferrule end as a guide. As the painted line thins, lift the brush off the tray to

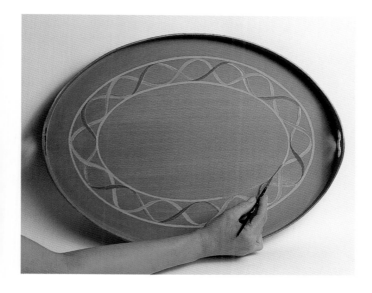

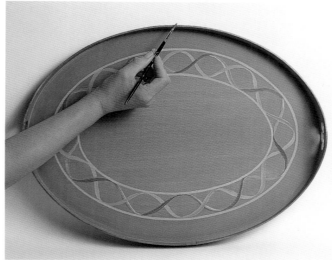

replenish the paint. Overlap the paint a little whenever you replace the lining brush on the surface. Continue in this manner until you have completed the oval line. Have a piece of damp clean kitchen paper handy for wiping away mistakes quickly. If this happens, simply dry the surface and begin again.

13. Repeat the process to paint the second border line only when the first is completely dry. Leave the second line to dry.

14. To make the antique gold-coloured paint for the edges of the tray, squeeze a little raw umber acrylic tube paint on to a jar lid and squeeze out the same amount of gold. Pour some water into the jar. Mix a little of the two paints together to make the antique gold, using more raw umber for the first coat. Use a

no. 3 artist's paintbrush to apply the antique gold to the top edge of the tray and around the handle cut-out shapes. Take great care not to stray over on to the green sides. Add more gold to the mixed paints for the second coat. Leave to dry completely.

15. When the tray is painted to your satisfaction, wipe away the chalk marks with slightly damp kitchen paper.

16. To give the tray the craquelure finish, sparingly apply an even coat of the oil-based ageing varnish to the tray, using a clean brush. Allow the varnish to dry overnight.

17. The next day, brush on the water-based crackle varnish sparingly. You will notice air bubbles or a foamy appearance and brushstrokes. To counteract

these, put down your brush and gently massage the surface with your fingers – this also helps the top coat to adhere well before it dries. Hold the tray up to an oblique light – if you can still see marks or "holes", dip a fingertip into a drop of washing-up liquid and massage it into the varnish before it dries. This should solve the problem. Leave for at least 1 hour or, better still, overnight.

18. Using a hairdryer switched to warm – not hot which would blister the varnish – apply a little warmth to the surface. Keep moving the hairdryer over the tray gently until you see minute, almost invisible, fine fissures appearing over the surface of the varnish.

19. To antique the cracks and make them show up well, mix a little raw umber oil tube paint in

a jar with some white spirit. Rub the paint into the cracked surface using kitchen paper or a brush to push the colour into the cracks. Wipe off the excess antiquing liquid with clean dry kitchen paper in a circular motion, until the paper is clean. Leave the tray to dry overnight.

20. Because the crackle varnish is water soluble the craquelure surface must be sealed with a coat of oil-based varnish before it can come into contact with moisture or water. Make sure the tray is completely covered with varnish and leave it to dry, according to the manufacturer's drying time. Apply a second coat of varnish to finish the tray. Once dry, the tray is ready to use.

Enamel towel holder & soap dish

A badly worn French enamel ladle holder is given a pretty paint finish to convert it into an ingenious stylish towel holder for use in a cloakroom, where space is often at a premium, or for displaying antique lace towels and extra special soaps for guests.

You will need

Old enamel ladle holder, scrubbed clean
Red oxide metal primer and old paintbrush
White acrylic primer undercoat
1in (2.5cm) household paintbrushes
Washing-up liquid
Matt emulsion paint in sage green and white (or use white artist's acrylic tube paint)
PVA glue
Old spoon
Plastic carton with lid
Lightweight gloves
Small natural sea sponge
Jam jar with lid
Artist's acrylic tube paint in gold
No. 3 artist's paintbrush
Semi-matt decorator's acrylic varnish

Old French enamel ladle holders similar to this one, which was showing signs of wear, had chipped edges and a little rust, are a good bargain compared to their pristine counterparts in mint condition.

1. Paint the ladle holder with the red oxide using an old brush. This creates a "key" on which to paint, as well as protecting against the return of rust. Watch for any runs in your paintwork and brush them out well. Leave to dry for about 1 hour.

2. Apply a second coat of red oxide, leaving it overnight to dry and set thoroughly.

3. Paint the ladle holder with two coats of acrylic primer undercoat, allowing the first coat to dry before applying the second. If the primed surface resists the paint, so that it separates and is patchy, add a drop or two of washing-up liquid to the paint to overcome the problem. Make sure that the whole surface is covered with paint, checking under the turned-up "bib-like" base, and the edges.

4. Apply a coat of the sage green paint. When dry, apply a second coat for dense all-over cover.

5. Mix a spoonful of the green emulsion with a spoonful of PVA glue and up to four parts water in a plastic carton to make a glaze. Place a spoonful of white emulsion or a small squeeze of white tube paint on the lid of the carton, using it as a palette.

6. Wearing gloves, dip part of the sponge into the green glaze, then into some of the white paint on the carton lid. Dab it on to the surface of the ladle holder at random, not in straight lines, replenishing the sponge with both colours as necessary, always picking up the glaze on the sponge first. Let the paint dry, before repeating this finish underneath and on the back of the ladle holder. (Wash out the sponge well afterwards, or the PVA glue will turn it rock hard.)

7. Fill the jar with water and squeeze a little gold tube paint on to the lid. Wet the no. 3 artist's paintbrush with water and mix into part of the gold. Begin painting simple scallop shapes, one at a time, along the edges of the ladle holder, keeping the scallops a consistent shape.

8. When the paint is completely dry, apply two coats of semi-matt decorator's acrylic varnish to finish, allowing the first coat to dry before applying the second.

Evening escapades

All the ideas incorporated in this section require a degree of concentration, but whichever project you choose you should find it sufficiently absorbing to "lose" yourself, thereby throwing off the pressures of the day. Many people find decoupage therapeutic, and gilding is a pleasant pastime with spectacular results. Have a good evening!

Rose-painted cachepot

Prettily shaped, good-quality cachepots are difficult to find but, once decorated, are ideal for displaying fresh flowers. Decorated in two and three tones, the colours used here were inspired by the delightful Renaissance-style fabric in the background.

You will need

Metal cachepot, degreased and
    scrubbed clean
Lightweight gloves
Fitch or small household paintbrush
Red oxide metal primer
White acrylic primer undercoat
1in (2.5cm) household paintbrush
Matt emulsion paint in pale pink or
    cream, dark pink and plum red
Jam jars with lids
Artist's acrylic tube paint in gold,
    raw umber and white
Nos. 2, 3 and 8 artist's paintbrushes
Pencil
Tracing of a suitable design
Low-contact masking tape
Artist's oil tube paint in raw umber
White spirit
Kitchen paper
Good-quality semi-matt
    oil-based furniture varnish
    or polyurethane lacquer
Self-adhesive suede

1. Wearing gloves, paint the cachepot inside and out with red oxide. Watch for runs on the edges and under the handles. Let dry for about 1 hour. Apply a second coat and leave overnight.

2. Paint the pot with acrylic primer undercoat, again watching for any build-up of paint on the top edges or runs under the handles. Apply a second coat for good cover and leave to dry.

3. Give the pot, inside and out, two coats of pale pink or cream emulsion paint, brushing it in one direction only and allowing the paint to dry between coats.

4. For the gold trim fill a jar with water, squeeze a little gold and some raw umber acrylic paint on to the lid. Mix together only a little of the colours with some water. Taking care not to stray on to the inside of the cachepot, paint the gold around the outside top edges of the pot and on to the handles using an artist's paintbrush. Allow to dry a little before applying a second coat.

5. Turn over your traced design and, using a pencil, go over the back of the lines showing through the tracing paper.

6. Turn the paper to the front and tape it on to the cachepot with masking tape. Repencil over the design to transpose the pencil on to the pot.

7. Using various artist's paintbrushes, paint the design in your chosen colours Leave to dry.

8. To age the cachepot make up some antiquing liquid by diluting a little raw umber oil tube paint with white spirit and apply it to the cachepot following the instructions on page 10. Start on the inside of the pot until you are sure about the colour – dilute the raw umber with more white spirit if necessary. Leave for 1–2 minutes before removing with kitchen paper. Repeat the process on the outside of the pot.

9. Leave to dry overnight without handling since any fingermarks will show. The next day, apply one coat of semi-matt oil-based furniture varnish. (An alternative option is to finish the cachepot with an antique craquelure finish – see page 11.)

10. Cover the base of the pot with self-adhesive suede, cut to fit, to give the pot a truly professional finish.

Country chest

When purchased, this little chest was covered in many layers of gloss paint, had long spindly legs and a few odd handles! Given a different shape, painted a charming green and treated to matching period handles, the chest now enjoys a new lease of life.

You will need

*Chest of drawers, fully stripped,
    sanded to a smooth finish and
    dust removed*
Shellac varnish and old paintbrush
White acrylic primer undercoat
1in (2.5cm) household paintbrushes
240 and 100 grade sandpaper
Matt emulsion paint in soft green
Set of drawer handles
Artist's oil tube paint in raw umber
White spirit
Kitchen paper
*Good-quality clear beeswax
    furniture polish*
Soft cloth

1. Make any repairs or alterations required – a new back cut in Medium Density Fibreboard (MDF) and wooden shaped angled pieces for the front and sides were glued and screwed in place to give this chest its new shape. Check that the drawers slide easily.

2. Remove the drawers from the frame and apply a coat of shellac varnish to the frame and drawers to create a barrier between stain remaining in the wood and the paint to be applied (see page 7). Try not to overbrush, as the shellac is fast drying and you will double the colour density, leaving dark patches. Apply a second coat when dry and leave to dry again.

3. Give the frame and drawers a coat of acrylic primer undercoat, diluted with a little water if it feels difficult to brush. Let it dry.

4. Sand the edges and surface of any MDF addition, which will feel rough after the painting, using the fine sandpaper. Apply another coat of primer and leave to dry.

5. Sand all the edges again and the top of the chest. Paint the chest in green emulsion, thinning the paint with a little water if necessary and brushing it in the direction of the grain. Let dry.

6. Give the chest a final coat of green and leave to dry, replacing the drawers but leaving them out of the frame a little so they do not stick when the paint dries.

7. Push the drawers in and touch up with a small brush any areas where colour is missing. Pull the drawers out again slightly until the paint dries.

8. Next, attach the new handles and "distress" the chest's paint-work. Working in the direction of the grain, sand the edges and areas where the chest would logically have suffered most wear over the years: under the handles, where the drawers would be pushed in and wear marks on the top. If the fine sandpaper is

unsatisfactory, use 100 grade paper. Distress the wood as much or as little as you like. There is no more painting to be done, so stain left in the wood is no longer a problem. Remove the dust.

9. The next step is to antique the outside of the chest, using raw umber oil tube paint mixed with white spirit and following the technique on page 10. Begin on one side of the chest at the top and brush on the antiquing liquid in the direction of the grain, using a household paintbrush. Leave for 5–10 minutes then start removing with kitchen paper. When the whole piece is finished, leave the chest untouched overnight to dry thoroughly.

10. After a day or two, apply beeswax polish generously to the chest. Leave for 10–15 minutes then buff up with a soft cloth.

Medieval-style cushions

The sparsely furnished interiors of grand medieval houses provided the ideal background for colourful tapestries, wall hangings and luxurious cushions in richly coloured damasks and velvets such as these. Warm yellow ochres, siennas and greens were the colours typically used in the Middle Ages.

GOLD VELVET BOLSTER

You will need

Tape measure
28 x 19in (71 x 48.5cm) rectangle of gold velvet, plus two 28 x 6in (71 x 15cm) strips for the ends
Iron
Scissors
19in (48.5cm) of ³⁄₄in (2cm) touch-and-close tape
Pins
Sewing machine
2³⁄₄yd (2.5m) of 1in (2.5cm) braid, or 5¹⁄₂yd (5m) narrow braid used in double rows
30in (76cm) strong piping cord or unbreakable string
2 small safety pins
2 large 6in (15cm) long decorative tassels
Matching thread and needle
5ft (1.5m) decorative cord
17in (43cm) long bolster or a cushion rolled to fit

Colourful braids, edgings, cords and tassels add a sense of occasion and grandeur to soft furnishings as these cushions ably demonstrate. Raid your own collection of remnants or invest in a little inexpensive finery to give these stunning results.

1. Turn under ³⁄₄in (2cm) on the two shorter sides of the large rectangle of gold velvet and press gently. Separate the length of touch-and-close tape and pin a length to each of these sides, one on the right side of the fabric and the other on the wrong side, so that they meet up when the fabric is rolled into a tube shape. Machine stitch in place.

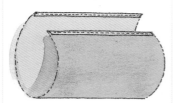

2. With the right side of the velvet uppermost, divide the rectangle into measured sections of about 5¹⁄₄in (13.5cm), to run the length of the bolster. Mark out the areas using pins on either side of the edges of the fabric. Cut the braid to length and pin along these lines in single or double rows, as preferred. Using thread to match the braid, machine stitch along the centre of each strip of braid, or along the sides if using wide braid. Attach a piece of braid above the touch-and-close tape that is stitched on the underside, if liked.

3. Take the two narrow strips of velvet, turn in 1in (2.5cm) along one long side of each piece to make the casing for the piping cord. Pin and machine stitch.

4. With right sides together, lay the unstitched long edges of these strips against the outside edges of the braided centre piece. Pin the panels in place and machine stitch 1in (2.5cm) from the edges, securing the ends of the touch-and-close tape in the stitching, and leaving a gap of about ³⁄₄in (2cm) in both lines of stitching a short distance from one of the touch-and-close tape strips. (This is for the raw ends of the decorative cord to be pushed through later.)

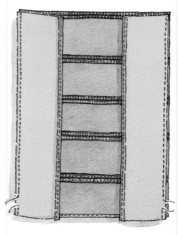

5. Cut the length of strong piping cord or unbreakable string in half to give two pieces. Attach one end of the first length of cord to a small safety pin and thread it through the casing on one of the side panels. Secure the cord temporarily with the safety pin. Repeat the process to thread the cord through the casing on the other side in the same way.

6. With right sides together, fold the bolster cover in half and pin the short ends of the side panels together. Machine stitch 1in (2.5cm) from the edges, as far as the casing seam line only, so as not to catch the piping cord in the machine stitches.

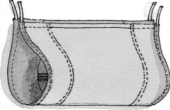

7. When these short ends of the panels have been stitched, pull the piping cord tight to gather the velvet and form the ends of the bolster. Knot the cord securely and trim the loose ends.

8. Holding the decorative tassels, pass your hands through the touch-and-close tape opening into the inside-out bolster cover. Pass the looped cord on the top of each tassel through the opening at each end of the bolster cover. Secure the tassels as part of the hand stitching needed to sew up the gathers securely and close the holes at both ends of the bolster. Any large or ugly stitches should be on the inside.

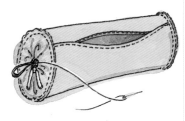

9. Turn the bolster cover the right side out. Hand sew the decorative cord around both ends to accentuate the circles. At each end of the bolster cover push the two raw ends of the cord through the small gaps left earlier. Secure with a few hand stitches. Insert the bolster or a cushion rolled to fit.

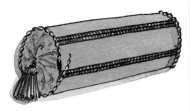

OVAL VELVET BOLSTER

You will need

28 x 21in (71 x 53.5cm) rectangle of brown velvet, plus two 9½ x 8in (24 x 20.5cm) rectangles for the ends
Tape measure
Pins
Scissors
56in (142cm) of 2½in (6.5cm) braid
Sewing machine
42in (107cm) of ¾in (2cm) touch-and-close tape
Matching thread and needle
56in (142cm) decorative cord
19-20in (48.5-51cm) long bolster or a cushion rolled to fit

1. Lay before you the larger rectangle of brown velvet with the right side uppermost. Measure about 6in (15cm) in from both long edges and mark with pairs of pins placed opposite each other to divide the panel into three.

2. Cut the wide braid into two equal lengths and pin these in place on the velvet rectangle in line with the pins so as to leave a 6in (15cm) wide centre panel in the rectangle, assuming your braid is 2½in (6.5cm) wide – otherwise adjust accordingly. Using thread to match the braid, machine stitch neatly along the edges of the braid to attach it to the velvet.

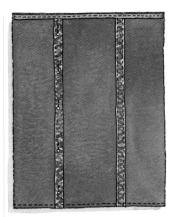

3. Turn under 1in (2.5cm) on the two shorter sides of the velvet rectangle. Cut the length of touch-and-close tape in half and pin a length to each of these sides, one on the wrong side of the fabric and the other on the right side, as for the Gold Velvet Bolster, so that they meet up when the fabric is rolled into a tube shape. Machine stitch the tape in place.

4. From the smaller pieces of velvet, cut two ovals measuring 9½ x 8in (24 x 20.5cm).

5. Roll up the braided velvet rectangle into a tube with the wrong side outermost, remembering to leave the touch-and-close tape open. Pin an oval in place at each end of the tube with the right sides together.

6. Machine stitch around each oval, 1in (2.5cm) from the edges, leaving a small gap of about ¾in (2cm) near the touch-and-close tape, to enable the ends of the decorative cord to be pushed through to the inside of the cover later. Machine stitch through the ends of the touch-and-close tape to secure it in place.

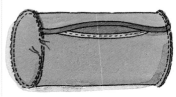

7. Turn the bolster cover the right side out. With neat stitches hand sew the decorative cord around the ends of the bolster to accentuate the ovals. Push the raw ends of the cord through to the inside through the gap that has been left and hand sew to secure. Insert the correct size bolster or a cushion rolled to fit.

SILK DAMASK CUSHION

You will need

Scissors
20 x 14in (51 x 36cm) rectangle of sea-green silk damask for the cushion cover back, plus 20 x 12in (51 x 30cm) rectangle for the front
Tape measure
Iron (on a silk setting)
Pins
Matching thread and needle
Zipping cut to 22in (56cm)

Sewing machine
4 gold key tassels
45in (114cm) chenille cord
18 x 10in (46 x 25cm)
cushion pad

1. To make the cushion cover back, cut across the wider rectangle of silk damask lengthways in order to create two pieces, one about 4¼in (11cm) deep and the other 9¾in (25cm).

2. Turn under 1in (2.5cm) on the two edges you have just cut and press. Pin then baste the zipping between these two pressed edges, leaving one end of the zipping protruding by about 2in (5cm). Machine stitch the zipping in place.

3. Open the protruding end of the zipping by about 1in (2.5cm) and cut a "V" shape down into the teeth so that the pointed ends of the fabric are longer (see page 60). This gives something to hold on to while you slide the zip opener on to one line of "teeth". Push the teeth of the other side into the opener and slide the opener within the rectangle of silk damask by about 1½in (4cm). Trim the zipping in line with the edge of the fabric.

4. Take the other rectangle of fabric and, with its right side uppermost, attach a key tassel to each corner, pinning them to the fabric by the looped cord on top of each tassel. Ensure each tassel

faces inward to the centre of the rectangle with its loop hanging out over the edge of the fabric.

5. With the zip partially open, and with right sides together, pin the two pieces of the cushion cover together. Machine stitch around the edges, leaving a 1in (2.5cm) seam allowance.

6. Turn the cushion cover the right side out. Hand sew the chenille cord on to the front in a decorative rectangular shape. Overlap the two ends of the chenille cord and oversew to avoid any fraying. Insert the cushion pad.

Carved candlesticks

These tall and elegant wonderfully carved candlesticks have been decorated in two colours, before being gilded with silver transfer leaf and then antiqued to give the appearance of the much-sought after silver gilt.

You will need

2 wooden candlesticks
Matt emulsion paint in turquoise and terracotta
Small paintbrushes or fitch
Acrylic gold size and small brush
Book of silver transfer leaf
Small soft brush
White spirit and kitchen paper, or fine wire wool
Spirit-based lacquer in mid-oak
White polish or shellac varnish
Optional wax finish: liming wax and artist's oil tube paint in viridian green and Payne's grey
Small bristle brush

You will notice that after the first three pictures were taken, I chose to reverse the colours on the base and top of the candlesticks.

1. First paint the plain uncarved parts of the candlesticks in turquoise and let the paint dry. Apply a second coat (and a third if necessary) until the surface has a good finish. Allow to dry.

2. Brush terracotta paint on to all the carved areas. Allow to dry, before applying more paint, until there is a good all-over cover.

3. Brush the acrylic gold size on to all the areas to be gilded, ensuring you apply it to all the awkward areas. Leave for at least 15 minutes, until tacky.

4. Gently press a sheet of silver transfer leaf on to the gold-sized areas, smoothing your fingers over it until all of the silver has transferred to the surface, leaving only the backing paper. Slightly overlap the next piece and continue in the same way.

5. With a soft brush, gently smooth down the silver, stippling it into the awkward areas and removing frayed edges. If you have missed small areas with the gold size, it is possible to go over them again, but remember to wait at least 15 minutes before attempting to relay the silver leaf.

6. The distressing can be now done in one of two ways: brush with white spirit those areas of the raised gilded surfaces that would most logically be worn and tarnished and immediately wipe it off gently with kitchen paper. Alternatively, gently rub through the silver leaf with fine wire wool.

7. Retouch the paintwork if silver debris has spoilt any of the candlesticks' surfaces.

8. After 24 hours, brush a "transparent" lacquer in a mid-oak colour on to the gilded surfaces for the silver-gilt effect. Alternatively, for a plain silver look, simply apply a protective coating of white polish to the leaf or, for a slightly older effect, shellac varnish.

9. For the soft, velvety look of the "verdigris" liming wax, mix a teaspoon of the wax with the paints to a shade you like. Brush the wax on with a bristle brush and leave overnight to harden. Buff up the wax or leave the finish dull-looking – as here.

Edwardian ewer & bowl

The soft cream and ochre colours of a parchment finish, applied to this enamel ewer and bowl using a small natural sea sponge, blend beautifully with the decoupage design of old parchment and yellow roses. The hand-painted trimming in antique gold gives a professional finishing touch to the enamel set.

You will need

Tall enamel jug and enamel bowl,
*   scrubbed clean and dried*
Red oxide metal primer
1in (2.5cm) household paintbrushes
White acrylic primer undercoat
Washing-up liquid
Matt or silk emulsion paint in cream
*   and white (optional)*
Old spoon
PVA glue
Plastic carton and lid
Artist's acrylic tube paint in white,
*   yellow ochre, gold, raw umber*
*   and Venetian red*
Small natural sea sponge
Kitchen paper
Lightweight gloves
Jam jar with lid
No. 3 artist's paintbrush
Small sharp pointed scissors
2 sheets good-quality floral
*   wrapping paper*
Reusable adhesive
White chalk
Pasting board
Small pasting brush
Ready-mixed heavy-duty
*   wallpaper paste*
Craft knife
Tack cloth
Acrylic lacquer suitable for
*   decoupage*

Old Edwardian ewers and bowls are becoming extremely hard to find in good condition – the bowls usually have ugly chips and rust around the rim and base. If you do find an antique jug with elegant lines, marry it with a large new bowl. Once the two share the same paint finish and design their different origins will be unnoticeable.

1. Paint the outside of the jug with red oxide metal primer. The simplest way to paint a tall jug is to push your arm inside it. Turn it as you paint, checking for runs underneath the handle and at the top where it joins the neck. Paint the jug inside as far as the neck seam and paint the inside of the bowl. Leave them both to dry for

about 1 hour, before turning them upside down to paint the underneath. Leave to dry again.

2. Apply a second coat of red oxide to the jug and bowl in the same way. Leave to dry overnight.

3. Paint the jug and the bowl with two coats of primer under-coat, allowing the first coat to dry before applying the second. If the paint resists or separates, a drop or two of washing-up liquid will solve the problem.

4. Paint the jug and bowl as before, with two coats of cream emulsion. If the paint feels difficult to brush, or brush marks spoil the surface, thin the paint with a little water.

5. Make up an emulsion glaze by measuring a tablespoon of PVA glue into the base of a plastic carton. Add a tablespoon of cream emulsion paint with up to four parts water. Mix well.

6. On to the carton lid tip a little white emulsion paint, or squeeze out a 1in (2.5cm) line of white acrylic tube paint and the same amount of yellow ochre. Squeeze out the sea sponge in clean water to soften it, then squeeze it a second time in kitchen paper to remove excess water.

7. Wearing gloves, dip the tip of the sponge into the cream glaze, before picking up the yellow ochre, then sponge in diagonal lines across the jug's surface.

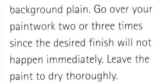

8. Continue sponging in this way, always dipping the sponge into the glaze first, before picking up the other colours to sponge on to the surface. Build up the sponged effect gradually in layers leaving some areas of the cream

background plain. Go over your paintwork two or three times since the desired finish will not happen immediately. Leave the paint to dry thoroughly.

9. Sponge the bowl inside and out in the same way as the jug. (Remember to wash the sponge out quickly when you have finished as the PVA glue will harden and make it rock-like.)

10. Fill the jam jar with water. On to the lid squeeze a little acrylic tube paint in gold and raw umber. Using the no. 3 artist's paintbrush, mix only a little of these together with a few drops of water to make an antique gold colour, using slightly more umber for the first coat.

11. Use the antique gold to paint around the rims of the jug and bowl, always painting in the same direction, replenishing the paint when necessary. Have by you a

piece of damp kitchen paper to wipe away any mistakes quickly. Continue until the gold covering is dense and the brushstrokes no longer show.

12. Replenish the antique gold-coloured paint on your "palette" and also a little extra raw umber. Paint the leaves, bows and the twisted ribbon using antique gold and raw umber, following the techniques on page 128. Finish the design by painting berries next to the leaves in Venetian red.

FOR THE DECOUPAGE

13. Using sharp pointed scissors, accurately cut out flowers and leaves for the decoupage from the floral wrapping paper, cutting a little deeper into each one, rather than leaving any background showing. Hold the paper in a relaxed fashion and turn the paper and not the

scissors as you cut in and out of serrated petals and leaves, always cutting in the same direction so as to have natural flowing lines. Complicated curling stems can be cut into two or three pieces and carefully butted together to become a complete stem again when pasted on to the surface.

14. When you have cut out a good pile of paper flower and leaf motifs, you can begin to create the design. Play around with the cut-outs on the surface of your jug and bowl, using reusable adhesive to hold them in position, until the picture looks balanced in shape and colour.

15. Once you are completely satisfied with the design, carefully chalk around the outside edges of the cut-outs in order to mark the outline of the shapes on to the surface of the jug and bowl. This helps you replace them in the correct place when they have been pasted. Where you are overlaying one piece of paper with another, remove the uppermost cut-out so as to reveal the underneath layer of shapes and chalk around those outlines as well.

16. Begin the pasting by removing the underneath pieces from the outside edge of the design, one by one. Select the first cut-out, turn it face down on to the pasting board. Brush paste over the cut-out, working from the centre outwards, spreading it evenly over the entire surface and making sure that the edges are covered. Carefully lift the cut-out off the pasting board, using your craft knife if necessary, and reposition it on the jug or bowl within the chalk marks.

17. Working from the middle of each cut-out outwards, smooth the paper down on the surface and eliminate any air bubbles, blemishes and excess paste with your fingers, dipping them in a little water if you find it helps since there is less likelihood of tearing the paper with slightly wet fingers. Carefully remove any excess paste with damp kitchen paper. Leave the real cleaning up until the paper has dried out when it will be stronger. When your fingers become sticky, rinse them occasionally in water otherwise they will remove the print from the surface of the paper. When each cut-out is in

position and absolutely flat, press the edges down well.

18. Leave the decoupage to dry once you have finished pasting.

19. Dampen kitchen paper or a small sponge slightly with warm water and use it to clean paste from the surface of the paper design, always working gently from the centre outwards. Then clean off the background, taking

care not to scuff the edges of the paper. If there are any loose edges, paste these down and clean up carefully straight away.

20. Hold the jug or bowl up to an oblique light and check closely that all the paste has been removed from the decoupage design and that the work is clean and ready for varnishing. Use a tack cloth to remove all traces of dust from the surfaces.

21. Apply acrylic lacquer to the jug and the bowl in the same way that you painted them. Brush the lacquer on evenly, always working in the same direction, watching for drips and runs. Leave it to dry. Apply a minimum of five coats of the lacquer – preferably more – to protect the surfaces and to give a lovely finish. The design should cease to appear "stuck on", taking on a wonderful depth.

Same-day sensations

Even with today's fast pace of living, we are still influenced by the furnishings and decorations inherited from bygone eras. Keep your eyes open for odd chair frames, small chests of drawers and old dressing tables, which may have been overlooked due to damage or their dark-stained appearance. Imagine them with a prettily shaped back and "skirt" or painted in pastel shades. Have a go at designing a pattern to paint yourself; find a good upholsterer – better still, join a class yourself!

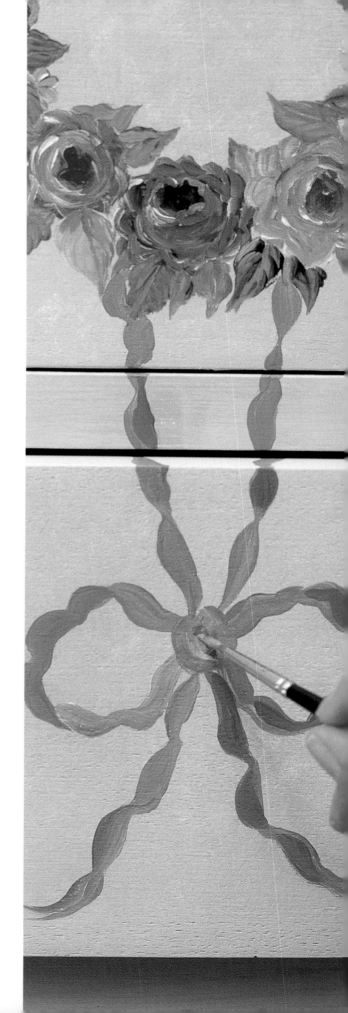

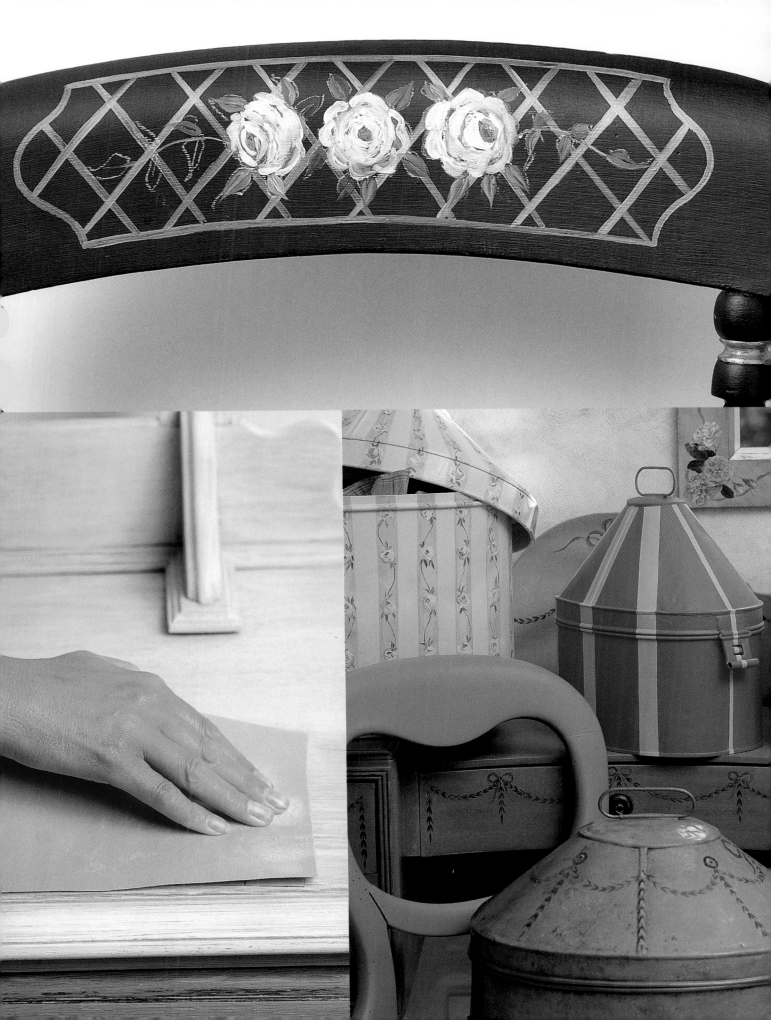

Black Victorian chairs

These two odd chairs have been painted black in true Victorian style and decorated with vibrant yellow roses, which are also reflected in the upholstery fabric on the seats. In all their new finery the chairs would look well anywhere in the house – in a vibrant modern setting or as part of a more classical theme.

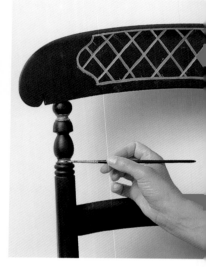

You will need

Wooden chairs, already stripped
100 grade and 240 grade sandpaper
Dust sheet or polythene
Shellac varnish and old paintbrush
Matt emulsion paint in black/
    nearly black
1in (2.5cm) household paintbrush
White chalk
Kitchen paper
Rule or straight edge
Plastic carton with lids
Artist's acrylic tube paint in raw
    umber, gold, yellow ochre,
    white, cadmium yellow medium,
    Hooker's green and Payne's grey
Nos. 2 and 4 artist's paintbrushes
Lining brush
Decorator's acrylic varnish or
    acrylic lacquer suitable for
    decoupage, or an oil-based
    varnish

Always look out for odd chairs or frames when searching through secondhand shops or antique markets. Although the two pictured here were purchased from different sources and are constructed from different woods, they are a similar shape and once painted the differences are minimal. These two chairs were stripped by hand, using a proprietary stripper specifically for removing varnish. An alternative would have been to have them professionally stripped.

1. Your chairs will probably feel rough to the touch after the stripping and will require sanding. Sand them with 100 grade sandpaper, always working in the same direction as the grain

in the wood. Progress to the fine sandpaper for a good finish. Remove the dust.

2. If your chairs are a dark wood which may have been previously stained, it would be wise to seal them with shellac varnish. The shellac creates a necessary barrier, preventing any stain left in the wood from "bleeding" into the paint and causing an unsightly stain, which would otherwise happen no matter how many coats of paint are applied on top. Spread out a dust sheet or polythene on a table or working surface. Turn the chairs upside down on to the dust sheet and apply the first coat of shellac, trying not to overbrush (go back over what has already been brushed on)

too much. Let the shellac varnish dry – it is spirit-based and therefore fast drying, so will probably dry within about 1 hour.

3. Turn the chairs upright to finish the coat. Let it dry.

4. Apply another coat of shellac in the same way and leave to dry.

5. With the chairs upside down again, apply the first coat of black emulsion paint, turning them upright again immediately to complete this coat. Leave to dry before applying a second coat of emulsion in the same manner.

6. Following the shape of the back of each chair, chalk on the trellis design – drawing the outline first. If

you make a mistake the chalk can be removed with a piece of damp kitchen paper each time, until you get it right. Then, with the help of a rule or a straight edge, chalk a trellis pattern within the outline.

7. Pour some water into a plastic carton and use the lid as a palette, squeezing out on to it some raw umber and gold tube paints. With an artist's paint-brush, mix a little of the two colours together with a drop or two of water. Take up the lining brush and draw it through the antique gold-coloured paint, until it is evenly loaded.

8. Steadying your little finger on the edge of the chair back, lay the lining brush on to the chalked line, up to the ferrule. Pull the brush towards you, watching the ferrule end. Keep some damp kitchen paper handy in order to

wipe away any errors which will be very obvious on the black background. When the paint begins to run out, carefully lift the brush off to replenish it. Begin again in the same way, overlapping the line slightly. Once the outline and trelliswork is completed, go over the outline again if it needs tidying up. Allow the paint to dry thoroughly.

9. Using the same antique gold and a no. 4 artist's paintbrush, paint the mouldings on the back of each chair, the legs and the cross-pieces, for a decorative gilded effect, typical of the Victorian era.

10. Chalk three simple rose shapes – circles with one or two frilly bits around the outside – in the centre of the trellis designs. Then chalk fine stems either side of the roses, with six leaves on each and a few more leaves

scattered around the roses to balance the design.

11. To paint the roses, squeeze out a little of the yellow ochre, white, and cadmium yellow acrylic tube paints on to another carton lid and refill the carton with clean water.

12. Dipping your brush into the water occasionally so as to thin the paint as you work, load the larger artist's paintbrush (no. 4) with yellow ochre paint and use it as the base colour for the roses to fill in the chalk shapes.

13. Before the yellow paint dries, overpaint the roses with white paint, which will blend slightly with the ochre. It can also be effective to load your paintbrush with yellow ochre on one side and white on the other for a shaded effect as you paint the bulk of the roses.

14. Now squeeze out on to your palette very small amounts of Hooker's green and Payne's grey acrylic tube paint, and also more white paint if necessary. With the fine artist's paintbrush (no. 2) and using the Hooker's green, paint the finest leaf stems possible. Try flattening the brush on the side of the palette, by wiping the paint off one side of it to get a fine line. Then fill in the leaf shapes with more green paint.

15. To complete the leaves, mix together a tiny amount of Payne's grey with the Hooker's green and go over some of the leaves to shade them, dipping the brush into some of the white paint as well from time to time. Wash the brush, dip it into either the white or the green paint (depending on whether the leaf is to be in shade, or to be highlighted) and outline each leaf and mark in a few of the veins.

16. Strengthen the centre of the roses or parts of the yellow ochre with a little of the brighter cadmium yellow colour, adding another touch of white paint to highlight the rose petals. Leave the paint to dry.

17. To complete the paintwork, paint a bow with twisted ribbons on the lower bar of the chair backs, if liked, using the raw umber and gold tube paints again. The trick here is to paint the loops of the bow and the tails in separate sections, which gives the twisted ribbon appearance.

Mix a little of the two colours together with some water first, using the no. 2 paintbrush. Wipe the brush on the edge of the palette and dip it into the raw umber; turn it over and dip the other side of the brush into the gold but do not overload the brush with paint. The two main loops of the bow are each

painted in three sections and you should start from the centre of the bow and work outwards to paint the right-hand loop first (see step-by-step photographs, page 129), beginning with the upper curve as follows.

Place the narrow tip of the brush on to the surface. Make a narrow, short fine line then a fuller brushstroke by pressing down on to the surface in an outward and upward movement, stopping just after the top of the first curve. Remove the brush from the work. Replenish the brush with paint as before and begin the lower curve. Starting from the centre again paint a fine line, then sweep the brushstroke out and round to beyond the bottom of the lower curve and stop. Dipping into the two paint colours again, start the third stroke from the end of the second line, pressing down on the bristles and then releasing

the pressure, to join up with the end of the first line, thereby completing the right-hand loop.

18. Paint the left-hand loop in the same way then do the smaller top loop in two or three stages also, finishing with a brush mark in the centre to represent the knot. Complete the bow by painting the tails to the sides. Do the same on the other chair.

19. If your chairs are to be upholstered professionally, ask the upholsterer specifically to take extra care. I always leave the work unvarnished until it returns, so that scuffs and marks can be touched up afterwards.

20. After the upholstering, remove any dust and fluff before applying two coats of acrylic varnish or an oil-based varnish to each, letting the first coat dry before applying the second.

Striped hat tin

A simple design of vibrant pink wide stripes on a paler pink background helps to smarten up an old military hat tin as it takes its place with others in this collection.

You will need

Domed military hat tin, stripped, sanded and degreased
Red oxide metal primer
Small fitch or paintbrushes
Shellac varnish and old paintbrush (optional)
White acrylic primer undercoat
Washing-up liquid
Matt emulsion paint in pale pink and bright pink
Pencil
Rule or straight edge
Low-contact masking tape
No. 8 artist's paintbrush
Semi-matt decorator's acrylic varnish or oil-based varnish

1. Remove any dust from the hat tin before painting. Make sure the lid opens easily before you begin by painting on the first coat of red oxide metal primer. Prop the lid open to let the primer dry – usually about 1 hour. Apply a second coat then leave overnight to dry thoroughly.

2. If you like, seal the red oxide with a coat of shellac varnish, which is fast drying.

3. Paint the tin with primer undercoat. If the paint separates in patches, add one or two drops of washing-up liquid to solve the problem. Let it dry, apply another coat and leave again to dry.

4. Paint the whole tin in pale pink emulsion, applying at least two coats, until you are satisfied with the all-over coverage.

5. Make sure the pale pink is absolutely dry – preferably leave it overnight – then mark out the stripes using a pencil and ruler. Quarter the tin first, then divide it up into eight sections.

6. Apply the masking tape in vertical stripes. Paint on the deeper pink. Let it dry a bit, before strengthening the colour. Again, apply as many coats as necessary to get a dense all-over cover. Leave to dry.

7. Remove the tape and touch up the paintwork as necessary if any paint comes away. If the edges are a bit "frilly" neaten up with an artist's paintbrush.

8. When the paint is dry, apply a good coat of semi-matt decorator's acrylic varnish or an oil-based varnish.

OTHER HAT TINS

The Lancer's hat tin on the chair was prepared in the same way as the striped one, then sponged in two or three similar colours, and decorated in a similar fashion to the Regency Desk (see page 126).

The decoration on the round bandbox tin was inspired by a 19th-century wallpaper. Painted in colours reminiscent of sugared almonds and marshmallows, and decorated with roses in complementary shades, it is impossible to recognize it for the sailor's hat-tin it once was.

The beautiful French hat tin in the café au lait-coloured stripes, was hand-painted with time-consuming tiny white rose buds. It looks marvellous with the French Cupboard (see page 46).

Victorian bedroom

The colour scheme for this little bedroom was inspired by the delightful Victorian-style fabric used for the walls and bedspread, and the hand-painted design on the chest of drawers and the chair back was adapted from the same fabric. The roses on the window-sill and the pretty bandbox add the final touch to the room.

CHEST OF DRAWERS

You will need

Small plain chest of drawers, already stripped, sanded and prepared for painting
White acrylic primer undercoat
1in (2.5cm) household paintbrushes
100 grade sandpaper
Matt emulsion paint in lavender, ivory and dark pink
Old spoon
PVA glue
Plastic carton and lid
Kitchen paper
Set of new drawer handles with an antique finish
Pencil
Tracing or greaseproof paper
Low-contact masking tape
Jam jar with lid
Artist's acrylic tube paint in deep violet, quinacridone violet, white, yellow ochre and light oxide green
Nos. 2, 3 and 8 artist's paintbrushes
Matt or semi-matt decorator's acrylic varnish
Good-quality clear beeswax furniture polish (optional)

This 1950s oak chest had a ply back and sides and its redeeming feature was the prettily shaped scalloped moulding which forms a "skirt" around the bottom. The chest's plastic handles were discarded and it was stripped of layers of gloss paint. To counteract the long spindly legs, a new back and sides were cut from MDF (Medium Density Fibreboard) in an undulating design to match the skirt.

If you wish to attach a new back and sides, the corner edges have to be mitred to form a frame, which should be "glued and screwed" to the chest. If the top is warped, there may be a gap showing under the new back frame, which will require filling.

1. Take your prepared chest and apply a coat of white primer undercoat all over, thinning the paint with a little water if it feels difficult to brush out. Let it dry.

2. Sand all the surfaces, paying particular attention to the edges of the top and drawers and any new MDF additions, which will have roughened up with the application of paint.

3. Remove the dust and apply a second coat of primer undercoat. Leave to dry. If the paint coverage is dense all over and looks good, move on to the lavender colour. If not, apply another coat of primer.

4. Paint the chest with lavender emulsion, always brushing it on in the direction of the grain. Let it dry, then apply another coat.

5. To make an emulsion glaze for soft stippling the chest, and later for sponging the chair, mix a tablespoonful of lavender and the same amount of PVA glue in a plastic carton with up to four parts water. Measure about a teaspoonful of ivory emulsion paint on to the carton lid.

6. Dip only the very tip of a paintbrush into the glaze, then into the ivory paint, and stipple the chest quite hard with the ends of the bristles so that they splay out. Turn the brush as you work to avoid a regimented look. The paint should not be too wet. Dry the brush on kitchen paper occasionally: there will still be sufficient colour on the brush. Stipple the whole chest or the top and drawers only. Replace the carton lid for later and place the brush in water to keep it soft.

7. Next, attach the new handles to the chest since it is always easier to work out a balanced design with the handles in place.

8. Using a pencil, trace a design from a favourite wallpaper or fabric on to tracing paper. Turn the paper over and go over the back of the lines showing through with the pencil. Turn the paper to the front once more, secure it in position on the top of the chest and with masking tape. Repencil over the design again to transpose the pencil markings on to the chest top.

9. Remove the tracing paper and strengthen the drawing by pencilling any lines that are unclear. Attach the traced design to the drawer fronts and use the same technique to transpose the design again.

10. Pour some water into a jam jar and squeeze a little of each of all the artist's acrylic tube paints on to the lid to use it as a palette – it is better to replenish the paints as necessary rather than have the colours dry out. If you have to leave the work, replace the lid – the water in the jar will ensure the colours stay soft.

11. Using artist's paintbrushes, start painting the design. Block in the rose shapes in the violet colours by painting a circular or ball shape with a few frilly bits around the edges for petals that have opened out. Before the paint is completely dry, and without washing the brush, pick up white paint on the tip of the brush and paint fine circles over the darker colours to shade them. Wash the brush then use neat white paint to highlight the outside of some of the petals. The roses will not "happen" immediately, they will have to

be worked on two or three times, in layers, until they begin to look realistic.

12. For the rest of the floral design, paint the daisies with yellow ochre then fill in the leaves with green paint, going back to pick up the neat white paint for shading, as before. Paint the veins and highlight some leaf edges, as appropriate.

13. Next, use a no. 2 artist's paintbrush to paint the twisted ribbons and bows on the chest, following the technique given on pages 128–129. Use two colours: dark pink emulsion and a second lighter pink derived from the dark pink lightened with a little white. Leave to dry thoroughly.

14. Using a no. 8 artist's paintbrush, apply the dark pink paint along the top edges on the back of the chest and on the skirt.

15. When the paint is dry apply two coats of decorator's acrylic varnish to the whole chest, letting the first coat dry, before applying the second. If you like, apply a good-quality clear beeswax polish to the surface, once the varnish is completely dry. Buff up well for a good shine.

BEDROOM CHAIR

As with the chest, the fresh, pale lavender background of this chair provides a perfect foil for the deeper, more vibrant colours of the decoration. The summery freshness of the lovely upholstery fabric enhances the chair and the double-corded self-trim around the chair seat gives a really professional finish.

Take a stripped and sanded chair frame and treat it in exactly the same way as the chest up to the paint finish stage, following Steps 1–4.

1. Then, wearing lightweight gloves, squeeze out a small natural sea sponge in clean water to soften it, then squeeze it a second time in kitchen paper to remove the excess water. Dip the tip of the sponge into the prepared emulsion glaze, then into the ivory paint on the carton lid. Sponge the chair all over, replenishing the sponge with glaze and then ivory, every now and then, until the chair looks good. (Wash the sponge out quickly in water, or the PVA glue will make it dry rock hard.)

2. Trace your design on to the back and front of the chair as you did for the chest of drawers, making sure the twisted ribbon on the back and the front "meets" on the top edge of the chair back.

3. Paint the design as before: use the dark pink emulsion to paint the mouldings on the chair back, legs and cross-pieces, as well as the bows and twisted ribbon. This time position a rose in the centre of the bow.

4. Once the paintwork is completed, have the chair frame upholstered carefully or do it yourself. Finally, apply two coats of acrylic varnish as before, to complete the chair.

Edwardian dressing table

This large and imposing piece of furniture initially appeared a big brute in its original dark brown stain but once stripped the possibilities became obvious. Decorated in an intense inky-blue colour to offset the white, and fitted with beautiful antique blue and white porcelain handles, it is now an attractive addition to a large sunny bedroom where extra storage space is welcome.

You will need

Similar piece of furniture, bleached, neutralized and sanded (see below)
Matt emulsion paint in brilliant white
Plastic carton
1in (2.5cm) household paintbrush
240 grade sandpaper
Low-contact masking tape
Jam jar with lid
Artist's acrylic tube paint in ultramarine blue and white
Kitchen paper
No. 8 artist's paintbrush
Good-quality clear beeswax furniture polish
00 grade flour paper
Soft cloth
Set of new drawer handles

The solidity and sheer size of this piece had somehow to be broken up without spoiling its clearly defined, elegant lines. It was decided to bleach the wood and then give it a white emulsion wash. Once dry, this paint finish was "floured in" to the beautiful oak grain to look like liming.

This method of "liming" wood is simple and quick, inexpensive and effective. In order for it to work, however, the wood must have a fairly open grain, as oak does, and must be well prepared – meaning that the wood needs to be clean and pale-looking.

To achieve this light and clean look, the mirror and all the handles from the drawer fronts were first removed from the dressing table and the piece was then stripped with a proprietary brand stripper, specifically formulated to remove dark stain and varnish.

Next the dressing table was sanded – first with an electric

low-contact masking tape in preparation for painting.

7. For the blue paintwork, fill a jam jar with water and squeeze a little ultramarine blue acrylic tube paint on to the lid of the jar. Have some kitchen paper handy to erase any mistakes quickly, should they occur since the blue paint will stain.

8. Dip a no. 8 artist's paintbrush into the jar of water then use it to stir around a little of the blue paint on the "palette" and thin it, before starting to apply the paint to the areas you would like to be blue – for example on mouldings, inside the mirror frame and in between the drawers. As you paint, dip the brush in the water from time to time. The paint looks rather like ink when it is watered down. It can be as pale or as intense as you choose. (In the step-by-step pictures you will notice there is a pale blue colour underneath the ultramarine. This is because I changed my mind, and decided the deeper colour would be more suitable than my original much paler blue.)

9. Finish the paintwork by painting a bow and twisted ribbons on the top of the dressing table back. The trick is to paint the loops of the bow and the tails in separate sections, which gives the appearance of twisted ribbon.

Replenish the ultramarine blue paint on your palette and

power sander fitted with 100 grade sandpaper, and then afterwards by hand so that particular care and attention could be paid to the mouldings and edges of drawers.

After removing the sanding dust, a proprietary furniture bleach was applied and the piece neutralized afterwards.

Always follow manufacturer's instructions when using furniture bleach, with regard to its application, timing and whether neutralizing is necessary. The piece then needs to be left to dry out thoroughly.

1. Remove the drawer handles and ensure your piece is dust-free by removing the drawers and vacuuming it thoroughly.

2. Tip some brilliant white emulsion paint into a plastic carton. Pour in a little water and stir well to thin the paint. Using a household paintbrush, apply the watery emulsion to the frame, brushing it on well in the direction of the grain of the wood.

3. Replace the drawers in the frame and paint them in the same way, until they are evenly coated. Pull the drawers out slightly from the frame when finished so that they do not stick as the paint dries. Leave the piece to dry thoroughly.

4. Using the 240 grade sand-paper and working all over the surfaces of the dressing table,

carefully sand the dried white paint into the grain in the wood, using an even pressure to avoid leaving a striped effect and working in the same direction as the grain. If you are not entirely satisfied with the look, apply more white paint evenly and allow it to dry, before sanding it into the grain once again.

5. Again using the fine sand-paper, rub through the paint to the wood on all the edges: on the frame, on the drawers, on the edges of the mirror frame and in other places where wear would logically be most apparent over the years.

6. To protect the glass, mask the edges of the mirror with

squeeze out a little white paint beside it. Mix a little of the two colours together with some water first, using a no. 8 paintbrush. Then wipe the brush on the edge of the palette and dip it into the blue; turn it over and dip the other side of the brush into the white but do not overload the brush with paint.

The two main loops of the bow are each painted in three sections and you should start from the centre of the bow and work outwards to paint the right-hand loop first (see the step-by-step photographs, page 129), beginning with the upper curve as follows.

Place the narrow tip of the brush on to the surface. Make a narrow, short fine line then a fuller brushstroke by pressing down on to the surface in an outward and upward movement, stopping just after the top of the first curve. Remove the brush from the work. Replenish it with paint as before and begin the lower curve. Starting from the centre again paint a fine line, then sweep out and round to beyond the bottom of the lower curve and stop. Dip into the two paint colours again and start the third stroke from the end of the second line, pressing down on the bristles and then releasing

the pressure, to join up with the end of the first line, thereby completing the right-hand loop.

10. Paint the left-hand loop of the bow in the same way then do the smaller loop at the top similarly, in two or three stages.

11. Finish with a heavy brush mark in the centre of the bow to represent a knot and paint the long tails of ribbon to the sides, which can run the width of the dressing table back.

12. Leave the paint to dry thoroughly before moving on to the next stage.

13. For a high degree of shine, apply a generous coat of clear furniture beeswax polish to the dressing table. Leave the wax to dry for about 10 minutes then take a sheet of 00 grade flour paper and sand the wax into the wood in the direction of the grain. Buff it up to a shine using a soft cloth.

14. Remove the masking tape from the mirror and replace the handles to complete the piece.

Weekend workovers

The simplest, most informally decorated room can be transformed by the clever use of colour. You may want the overall effect to be rustic and gentle, vibrant and colourful, soft, faded and elegant, or in shades reminiscent of the countryside. All of these possibilities are woven into this section. "Antique style" is all about creating an effect.

Medieval cupboard

Before the advent of fitted kitchens, a cupboard of this type would have been used for food storage and as an alternative working surface to the kitchen table. This piece was in a terrible condition when rescued from the local rubbish tip but is a perfect illustration of what can be achieved with a little imagination, a few pieces of new moulded skirting board and colourful paint!

You will need

Scraper
Strong craft knife
Similar cupboard, already stripped
100 grade sandpaper
Shellac varnish and old paintbrush
Matt emulsion paint in black/ nearly black, white,

peacock blue, deep inky-green and reddish brown
1in (2.5cm) household paintbrushes
Old spoon
Yellow ochre pigment powder
Small bowl
Ruler
White chalk
Nos. 8 and 4 artist's paintbrushes
Artist's acrylic tube paint in white (or use any emulsion paint), raw umber, gold, yellow ochre, Venetian red, cadmium red medium, crimson, ultramarine blue and rich gold
Jam jar with lid
Lining brush
Set of new handles
Semi-matt decorator's acrylic or an oil-based varnish

Narrow moulded skirting boards were added to the top and sides of the cupboard's front. Sheets of ply were then mounted on a shallow timber frame and fitted to give the cupboard false sides, for more width, before "gluing and screwing" wider pieces of skirting board to the base. The

style of the moulded board was chosen to match the ugly rounded edges on the cupboard, creating a double edge.

The black paint is a perfect background on which to paint a convincing medieval design and the trompe l'oeil "carved" mouldings of acanthus leaves break up the plainness of the black background. The rounded double mouldings on the sides of the cupboard are decorated in twisted gold to represent metallic wire or thread. This is also reflected in the tassels, since metallic thread was commonly incorporated in fine textiles – similar to that seen today in ecclesiastical embroidery used on altar cloths. The heraldic shield decoration, along with a lucky find of a set of rusty handles, give an authentic feel to the medieval look.

1. Using a scraper and a strong craft knife, scrape off and gouge out any remaining paint caught in nooks and crannies in the cupboard. Using 100 grade sandpaper, sand in the same direction as the grain. Sand any new ply along the edges which may be

rough from cutting. Ensure all doors open easily and scrub the cupboard clean.

2. If the cupboard is dark-stained, apply two coats of shellac varnish to act as a barrier between any wood stain and the paint to be applied (see page 7). Allow the first coat of shellac to dry before applying the second.

3. Paint the cupboard in black/ nearly black emulsion, leaving the doors ajar afterwards and opening out the foldaway working surface, so that you can paint the edges and that they can dry without sticking. Similarly, remove any drawers or at least pull them out a little.

Give the cupboard several coats, allowing the paint to dry each time, until the all-over coverage is densely black and the paintwork looks good.

4. Open up the cupboard so as to paint the interior. Carefully empty a tablespoon of ochre pigment (taking care not breathe in the fine powder) into a small bowl and mix with a little water. Add three or four tablespoons of

sections and make a chalk mark about every 6–8in (15–20.5cm). Within these areas chalk a series of acanthus leaves. Do the same along the mouldings at the top and the base of the cupboard, working outwards from the middle of each to ensure a balanced design.

6. Using a no. 8 artist's paintbrush, paint the basic leaf shapes in peacock blue emulsion.

7. The idea of trompe l'oeil is to give a three-dimensional effect which deceives the eye into believing it is the real thing, and the shading is part of this trick. You must therefore decide which side of the cupboard is going to be in shade, and which is to be highlighted. Then begin shading the leaves on the darker side with

the deep inky-green emulsion paint (or use black mixed into the peacock blue paint).

8. Add a little white tube or emulsion paint to the peacock blue and use this to highlight areas on the opposite sides. Stand back to look at the effect. Go back to it several times, making the shaded and highlighted areas pronounced.

9. Chalk in the lines of twisted wire on the mouldings, ensuring they meet neatly at the corners of the mouldings.

10. Pour some water into a jam jar and squeeze out a little raw umber and gold acrylic tube paint on to the lid. Mix a little of the two colours together with a drop or two of water.

white emulsion paint to the watery mixture, stirring it thoroughly. Adjust until the colour is intense. Paint the interior of the cupboard, taking particular care on the front edges

where it joins the black. When it is dry apply another coat. Touch up any black paint as necessary.

5. Roughly measure the side mouldings on the cupboard into

paint by absorbing it, so it will be necessary to replenish the brush with paint every so often. Overlap the paint slightly when you return the brush to the line. Continue until the two edging lines all around the cupboard (except for the base where there is only one) are finished. Leave the gold paint to dry and fit all the new handles.

12. For the heraldic shield design, divide the foldaway front piece in half vertically with a ruler and make a fine chalk mark. Measure about 4in (10cm) down from the base of the handle and make a mark – this will be the middle of the top of the shield. Elongate the central line 9in (23cm) to the point of the shield. Chalk the shape freehand. Using the ruler, divide the shield into the four sections. Draw the rest

of the design freehand, erasing mistakes and redrawing until you are satisfied with it.

You can see from the photograph which colours were used here, or choose your own. Shade the tassels in the same way as the trompe l'oeil leaves. Block in the vibrant red and blue of the shield, going over the paint a few times until the colour is dense and the brush marks are less obvious. Once the "fabric" design is finished, and over-painted with reddish brown leaves, load the lining brush with the rich gold. Line the shield and the metallic thread on the ropes and tassels and in the fabric.

13. To complete the cupboard, apply two coats of varnish all over, allowing the first coat to dry before applying the second.

11. Take up the lining brush, pull it through this mixture once or twice, until the brush is evenly loaded. Beginning at the top of one side moulding, carefully lay

the brush on the chalked line up to the ferrule. Pull it towards you (downward in this case), following the twisting chalk line. The chalk will quickly dry the

Roses headboard

Sumptuous old parchment roses are formed into a beautiful decoupage garland to decorate a new Medium Density Fibreboard (MDF) headboard, painted in the colours of faded linen or old chintz. This design blends well with other floral patterns in the room and the crisp old linen sheets on the bed complete the antique style.

You will need

MDF framed headboard
White acrylic primer undercoat
1in (2.5cm) household paintbrushes
100 grade and 240 grade sandpaper
Matt emulsion paint in ivory, cream, fudge and light brown
Old spoon
Plastic carton with lid
PVA glue
Artist's acrylic tube paint (or any emulsion paint) in white
Small natural sea sponge
Kitchen paper
Lightweight gloves
No. 8 artist's paintbrush or narrow fitch, ³⁄₈in (1cm) wide
Small sharp pointed scissors
4 sheets good-quality floral wrapping paper depicting roses, buds and leaves
Ruler or tape measure
White chalk
Reusable adhesive
Pasting board
Pasting brush or ½in (1.5cm) household paintbrush
Ready-mixed heavy-duty wallpaper paste
Craft knife
Small container or jar lid filled with water
Tack cloth
Semi-matt acrylic lacquer suitable for decoupage

If you have a non-yellowing oil-based varnish in the house, it could be used as an alternative to the acrylic lacquer, but do test the colour on the bottom of the headboard first where it will be concealed by the pillows. If you are satisfied that it is not too dark, apply it sparingly to the decoration since the pale flowers will absorb the colour of the varnish. It would be best, however, to apply two coats of acrylic lacquer first. Follow the manufacturer's instructions for drying times.

For an aged look, you could apply a craquelure varnish (see page 11) after first applying two coats of water-based acrylic lacquer to seal and protect the decoupage paper design.

1. Paint the headboard, back and front, and the frame with white primer undercoat, thinning the paint with a little water if necessary. Leave it to dry well.

2. Using the 100 grade sandpaper, sand all the surfaces, in the direction the grain would be if it were wood: across for the surface and top of the frame,

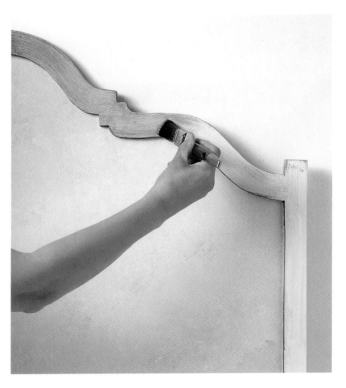

vertically for the uprights. Pay particular attention to the MDF frame, as the application of paint will have roughened it up. Work on it until it feels smooth.

3. Remove the dust before applying another coat of white primer undercoat, again thinned with a little water if it is too thick. Allow to dry.

4. Take the fine sandpaper and sand the undercoated frame once more, working on it until smooth (the edges can show through). Remove the dust.

5. Paint the whole of the headboard in ivory emulsion,

letting the paint dry thoroughly, before applying a second coat.

6. Make up an emulsion glaze by measuring about two tablespoons of ivory into the base of a plastic carton, with the same amount of PVA glue and up to four parts water. Mix thoroughly.

7. Use the carton lid as a palette and place on it a spoonful of cream emulsion, a teaspoonful of fudge colour and a tiny amount of both light brown emulsion and the white tube or emulsion paint.

8. Squeeze out the sea sponge in clean water to soften it, then squeeze it a second time in

kitchen paper to remove excess water. Wearing lightweight gloves, dip the tip of the sea sponge into the glaze, then into smallest possible bit of fudge-coloured paint. Using only the tip of the sponge to get the colour on, work diagonally to get the dark line or "vein" on to the headboard. You are not looking for "sponged" marks at this stage.

9. Dipping into the glaze first again, pick up the cream to apply it either side of the vein, working on it long enough to soften out the edges. Follow this with more glaze, then white, sponging over the vein to soften it and continuing until you are satisfied

with it. If you are not entirely happy with it, walk away from it, prop up the headboard and stand back and look! You will easily see exactly which areas need attention. Let the paint dry a little, before going over it again. The beauty of this paint finish is that you can alter the whole surface and change your mind – within reason! If it is too dark, add white or pale areas; too light – add shade. To achieve a wonderfully layered, three-dimensional look with great depth, you have to apply two or three "layers". Let the paint dry and wash out the sponge quickly in water or the PVA glue will make it rock hard.

10. Replace the carton lid – although the paint will probably fall into the glaze it does not matter, you may need it for touching up shortly.

11. With a no. 8 artist's paint-brush or a narrow fitch, shade the inside of the frame with watery light brown emulsion. Pull the brush over the frame to get a roughly dragged finish. You may need to shade it twice. One side can be "in the light", the other in shade and therefore darker. Remove any brown paint that strays on to the cream paint finish with damp kitchen paper.

12. Go back to the 1in (2.5cm) brush and paint the remainder of the frame, including the outside edges, with the fudge colour, again "dragging" the diluted paint. Only the smallest amount on the tip of the brush is necessary. You should be able to pull the brush through the fudge colour, time after time, until the lines of the dragging look good. If it dries out before you have finished, dip the tip of the brush into the paint and start again. Let it dry. Shade parts of the frame with the light brown paint, dragging it almost dry, in areas that be in the shade.

13. Using the same technique, apply the white paint almost dry – by dipping the tip of the brush into the paint, wiping it on kitchen paper first if it is too wet. This gives the frame a limed appearance – all adding to the rustic look! Leave to dry.

FOR THE DECOUPAGE

You will find it easier to design the decoupage with the head-board in an upright position. It can be laid down later for pasting if preferred.

14. Using sharp pointed scissors, cut out a large selection of roses and an even larger variety of leaves from the wrapping paper (see page 84 for the cutting-out technique). Unsuitable leaves may be reshaped to look realistic. Cut out plenty of buds, too, choosing a few pieces with fine stems which can be used to taper off the garland at the ends and to add interest to the design.

15. Measure across and find the centre top of the headboard – this is where the most beautiful roses will go – and make a mark with white chalk.

16. When you have cut out a good pile of paper motifs begin to create the design. Using very small pieces of reusable adhesive, apply the main pieces of the design to the headboard first: the largest roses and leaves on the corners and in the centre. Gradually build up the design. Tuck leaves and stems under the roses, securing them in place with reusable adhesive. Once the outlines of the design are in place, stand back and look. Fill in the gaps with as many leaves as possible, remembering that in a real garland there would be more leaves than flowers, some falling naturally over the flowers. Fiddle with the design until it looks well balanced, and you are satisfied with it. Stand back at a distance for one last check.

17. Carefully chalk around the outside edges of the cut-outs so that the shapes are marked on the surface (as long as the chalk shows up sufficiently). This will be helpful for replacing them in the design when you have pasted them.

18. Lay the headboard down on to a comfortable working surface. Always begin with those cut-outs that are underneath the others, and work upwards to the uppermost ones. Usually this will also mean working from the outside of the design towards the middle. Remove one piece at a time from the board, remove the reusable adhesive and place the cut-out upside down on the pasting board.

19. Brush paste over the cut-out, working from the centre of the motif outwards, spreading the paste evenly over the entire surface and making sure that the edges are covered. Carefully lift the cut-out off the pasting board, using a craft knife if necessary, and replace it on the headboard within the chalk marks.

20. Working from the middle of each cut-out outwards, smooth the paper down on the surface and eliminate any air bubbles, blemishes and excess paste with your fingers, dipping them in a little water if you find it helps, since there is less likelihood of tearing the paper with slightly wet fingers. Carefully remove any excess paste with damp kitchen paper. (Leave the real cleaning up until the paper has dried out when it will be stronger.) When your fingers become sticky, rinse them occasionally in water otherwise they will remove the print from the surface of the paper. When each cut-out is in position and absolutely flat, press the edges down well.

21. When the pasting is completed, leave it to dry out, before cleaning up the surfaces of the paper and background well with damp kitchen paper.

22. Before applying the lacquer use a tack cloth to remove dust, wiping it carefully over the surface. Restick any edges that have lifted and press down.

23. Apply at least 10 coats, preferably more, of acrylic lacquer (it dries very quickly, allowing several coats to be done in a day), to lose the "stuck-on" look and give the work depth.

Indian coffee table

When purchased, this sturdy Indian table had suffered water damage on part of its top, which could not be erased by sanding. Instead this vibrantly colourful panel was painted on top, inspired by the intricate designs of Eastern carpets and painted to tone with the Exotic Suliman Silk Cushions (see page 58).

You will need

Wooden table
White spirit or 100 grade sandpaper
Shellac varnish and old paintbrush
Ruler
White chalk
White acrylic primer undercoat

½in (1.5cm) household
    paintbrush
Pencil
Tracing or greaseproof paper
Low-contact masking tape
Old plate
Matt emulsion paint and/or
    artist's acrylic tube paint

in vibrant colours, such as
    bright blue, jade green,
    purple, pink, orange, red
    and yellow ochre
Artist's acrylic tube paint in
    pewter
Nos. 7, 3 and 2 artist's
    paintbrushes

White polish (optional)
Methylated spirits
Good-quality clear beeswax
    furniture polish
Soft cloth

If you want to erase ugly white water marks from a polished piece of furniture such as a table first seek an estimate from a furniture restorer. Having followed this line myself and being informed one particular item was an impossibility, I decided to tackle it myself, with quite pleasing results!

To try it for yourself take a piece of fine 00 grade flour paper or the finest cabinet paper and sand the marked area carefully by hand, working in the direction of the grain in the wood. If the mark begins to shift, continue until it has decreased in size and the whiteness is fading. When you feel you should stop, apply a generous coat of good-quality clear beeswax furniture polish and leave it for 10–15 minutes to dry. With a new sheet of 00 flour paper or fine sandpaper, sand the wax by hand into the wood, again working only in the direction of the grain. Reapply another coat of the wax and leave it to dry, before buffing up with a soft cloth.

If you have tried to erase such a water mark and there is no hope for your table, an alternative is to jazz it up with a vibrantly coloured design like the one used here. You can use either brightly coloured matt emulsion or acrylic tube paints for the table top but the former will require several coats to eradicate the brushstrokes and to match the depth and brilliance achieved by using tube paints.

1. If your table has wax polish on the surface, this must be removed first. To remove the wax rub the table top with white spirit or sand it with 100 grade sandpaper, or finer, only ever working in the direction of the wood grain. By sanding the table top you will remove the waxy shine and create a good "key" on which to paint.

2. An application of shellac varnish is the next step in preparing the table. The shellac is necessary to create a barrier, preventing any stain left in the wood from "bleeding" into the paint to be applied and causing an unsightly stain, which would otherwise happen no matter how many coats of paint are applied on top.

Paint the surface of the table top with two coats of shellac varnish, using an old brush. Let the first coat dry thoroughly, before applying the second. Try not to go back over the shellac that has already been brushed on, once it is spread out since over-brushing will double the colour density and create dark patches in the finish.

3. Once the shellac varnish has dried, use a ruler and chalk to mark out a suitably sized rectangular panel (or whatever shape suits your table) as the basis for your design.

4. Apply a coat of white acrylic primer undercoat to this panel and leave it to dry. Apply a second or third coat until the paint coverage is evenly white. Let it dry. This white undercoat provides a good base for showing up the colours to be used, rather than darkening them.

5. Next, design a decorative panel for your table top, using a pencil and tracing or greaseproof paper. You could use the outline

(opposite) as a guide – the idea for which was inspired by the many different shapes and motifs found in Eastern carpets – or trace a pattern from a favourite wallpaper or fabric or even create a freehand one of your own.

6. Turn the tracing paper over and go over the back of the lines showing through the paper in pencil. Turn the paper to the front once more and position it on top of the painted panel on the table top, securing it in place with low-contact masking tape.

7. Repencil over the whole design to transpose the pencil markings on to the table top. Do check from time to time that the design is showing up on the panel – it should show up well on the white painted background.

8. Remove the tracing paper and touch up the drawing as necessary so that all the pencil lines are clear.

9. Use an old plate as a palette and place a little of the required paints on to it – follow those bright colours used here or choose your own shades.

10. Begin to paint by filling in the design, using fine artist's paintbrushes (nos. 2 and 3) for smaller areas and fine lines, and a larger one (no. 7) for larger blocks of colour. Where colours are adjoining, let one paint dry before applying the next, so as to

keep the colours clearly defined and with no blurring of edges. The design will probably require several coats of each colour until the brush marks can no longer be seen so much and the shades all appear intense.

11. Finally, fill in the background colour and edge the panel with another colour (a rich purple and a pinky-red were used here). Stand back to check the impact of your painted table top. Make any amendments as necessary then leave the paint to dry.

12. Complete the painting by applying two coats of paint to the legs of the table in a colour to match the design – bright blue paint was used here.

13. To finish the table, apply a coat of white polish, which is pale shellac varnish, to seal the table top and legs. Or, if you prefer a more antique finish, use shellac varnish instead, perhaps diluted a little with methylated spirits. Whichever of these you use you will need to watch for runs on the edges since both are thin liquids. Leave to dry.

14. The following day, apply a good-quality clear beeswax furniture polish to the whole table, including the legs, and leave for 10 minutes. Then use a soft cloth to buff up the surfaces with plenty of gusto for a fabulous shine.

Singer sewing machine table

Originally, Singer sewing machines and their bases were made of iron and finished in black. This bright green is a more fun approach – inspired by the colour of verdigris – and the original top has been replaced by an attractively shaped one in Medium Density Fibreboard (MDF), which has been painted and sponged to look like marble.

You will need

Old Singer sewing machine table
Shellac varnish and old paintbrush
Wire brush
Red oxide metal primer
White acrylic primer undercoat
1in (2.5cm) household paintbrushes
Washing-up liquid
Old spoon
Matt emulsion paint in jade green,
    white and pale lime green
Small plastic cartons with lid
Small fitch
Old talcum powder
MDF top, 33 x 17in (84 x 43cm)
    at the narrowest point in
    the middle
Fine sandpaper
PVA glue
Small natural sea sponge
Kitchen paper
Lightweight gloves
Decorator's acrylic varnish

1. If possible, stand the Singer sewing machine table outside on a fine day so you can work on it properly and remove any dirt and dust from the ironwork on the base.

2. If the ironwork is black and still in good condition, simply seal the metal by using an old brush to apply a coat of shellac varnish, which is fast-drying. Leave the base to dry completely.

3. If the base is rusty, however, remove loose rust with a wire brush – while wearing goggles so as not to get any particles of rust in your eyes – before applying a coat of red oxide metal primer. Leave to dry for about 1 hour. Check the ironwork from all angles to ensure all the nooks and crannies have been covered with red oxide. Apply a second coat if you feel it is necessary and leave overnight to dry completely.

The next day give the table base two coats of acrylic primer undercoat, allowing the first coat to dry before applying the

second. If the first coat of the acrylic primer does not adhere well to the red oxide primer, a drop or two of washing-up liquid added to the paint should solve the problem.

4. Spoon out a small quantity of jade green emulsion paint into a plastic carton and a little white emulsion into another carton. Using a fitch, paint the iron base with the jade green, stippling on

the paint using the tip of the bristles. Really push the paint into the surface, the more uneven the effect, the better. Dip the tip of the brush into the white emulsion and add a shake of

talcum powder to the paint occasionally, to add to the texture. Continue in this way until the base is well covered. Leave the paint to dry.

5. Turn the base round, or walk around it to check for any unfinished areas. Touch up all the unpainted areas, paying special attention to the treadle, which has a more intricate design. Let it dry.

6. Lastly, give the Singer lettering and the other areas in the front that are most obvious, another coat of stippling to improve the colour and texture.

7. Now move on to the table top. Give the MDF top and edges a coat of acrylic primer undercoat, thinning it with a little water if necessary so the paint is easier to apply. Let it dry, before applying a second coat. When it has dried completely, the MDF will have roughened a little with the paint. Sand the top surface and the edges with fine sandpaper, until smooth. Remove the dust.

8. Turn the top over, paint the other side then sand it as before.

9. Paint the top and the edges in jade green emulsion, letting the first coat dry before applying a second. Allow to dry. Paint the other side in the same way.

10. Make up an emulsion glaze in a plastic carton, using one spoonful of jade green and one of PVA glue, mixed with up to four parts water. Spoon out a little white emulsion paint into another carton. Squeeze out the natural sea sponge in clean water to soften it, then squeeze it a second time in kitchen paper to remove excess water.

11. Wearing lightweight gloves, dip the sponge into the glaze, before dipping the tip of it into the white paint. Working diagonally, sponge the paint in wavy lines across the table top, making some areas lighter than others and leaving areas of the bright background to show through. When you are satisfied with the paint finish, let it dry a little. Spoon out some lime green emulsion on to a carton lid.

12. Remembering to dip the sponge into the glaze first, pick up some of the lime green paint and sponge this into "veins", to represent marble. Once you are satisfied with the lines of green, they can be softened by reapplying the original colours again, if you wish. Applying one or two layers gives a lovely three-dimensional appearance and greater depth. Bring the marbling lines and veins over the edges of the table top to make it look like real marble.

13. Wash the sponge out quickly in water or the PVA will turn it rock hard. Let the painted top dry completely before standing it on the base, and leave it for another day or two before applying one or two coats of decorator's acrylic varnish to finish.

Fabulous fireboard

As an alternative to an arrangement of flowers in an empty hearth, this fabulous trompe l'oeil lead urn, filled to overflowing with a magnificent array of decoupage blooms, greatly enhances any fireplace when not in use, as well as providing an attractive focal point for the room.

You will need

White acrylic primer undercoat
1in (2.5cm) household paintbrushes
Medium Density Fibreboard (MDF)
    fireboard
Plastic carton
Fine sandpaper or cabinet paper
Matt emulsion paint in a very dark
    colour for the background, such
    as navy blue, deep grey blue or
    darkest fir green; light brown
    (or use artist's acrylic tube
    paint in raw umber, mixed with
    white) and cream
White chalk

Rule or straight edge
Artist's acrylic tube paint in
    Payne's grey and white
    (or use matt emulsion
    paint black/nearly black
    and in white)
Nos. 7 and 3 or 4 artist's
    paintbrushes
Small sharp pointed scissors
4 sheets good-quality floral
    wrapping paper
Reusable adhesive
Pasting board
Small pasting brush
Ready-mixed heavy-duty
    wallpaper paste

Craft knife
Kitchen paper or small sponge
Tack cloth
Semi-matt acrylic lacquer
    suitable for decoupage

1. Apply a first coat of primer undercoat to both sides of the fireboard and its edges, stippling the paint into the edges with the tip of the paintbrush. If the paint feels too thick, tip it into a plastic carton and stir in a little water to thin it – this will make brushing it on much easier. Leave to dry.

2. Sand the whole surface of the fireboard, always working the sandpaper in the same direction. Pay particular attention to the edges, which will have roughened up with the application of paint. Tear off a small portion of the sandpaper and roll it up into a pencil shape, to get into the cut-out shapes on the edges of the fireboard. Remove the dust.

3. Apply a second coat of white primer undercoat all over the fireboard. Stand the board upright and let the paint dry.

4. Before covering the fireboard in dark emulsion paint in your chosen background colour, make a mental note of roughly where the top of the urn should begin. Paint the back of the fireboard and the top part of the front, brushing the paint outwards over the edges to avoid a build-up of paint. Catch any drips on the edges. "Draw" the urn's outline with the paintbrush by pulling the brush across the area where the top rim of the urn will be, using very little paint, so that the white undercoat shows through. Leave a narrow gap of white for the fluted rim (which will be highlighted later) around the top of the bowl and on the neck of the urn. Decide, as you paint, which side is to be highlighted and which is to be in shade for a

trompe l'oeil effect (see page 9). Then paint the dark colour down to the bottom of the fireboard and let the paint dry.

5. Apply a second coat of the background colour to the top of the front and the base area, the back and the edges of the board.

6. On the front of the fireboard, chalk the urn's basic design and use a rule or straight edge to outline the stone slab on which it rests (see picture, page 122).

7. Improve the shading with Payne's grey or black emulsion paint, using a no. 7 artist's paintbrush and only a little water to accentuate the black underneath the decoration on the top rim, under the bowl, and between the

neck mouldings, as well as on the side of the urn that is to be in the shade.

8. Use a little of the dark background colour mixed with white tube paint or emulsion to highlight the bowl and rims. Lighten the colour to apply it to the uppermost decoration. It is not necessary to wash your brush each time – the colours actually blend much better when you dip the brush from one shade to another. Wash the brush only when applying neat white paint.

9. Paint light brown emulsion and grey tube paint (or their equivalents) on to the front and side of the stone. Use light brown for the top of the stone, highlighting relevant edges in cream.

10. Use a fine artist's paintbrush (no. 3 or 4) to smarten up the paintwork, making sense of it all. Stand back and look at the urn. It will be immediately obvious where small alterations and additions need to be made. Any final highlighting of the urn can be done when the design is completed and to give it a three-dimensional effect. Now fill it with flowers!

FOR THE DECOUPAGE

Use the wonderful shape of the urn to the utmost advantage, remembering flowers do droop downwards – especially roses and other heavy blooms. The most fragile little flowers and buds can be pasted on last of all to fill in any gaps and balance the picture.

11. Using sharp pointed scissors, cut out masses of flowers and leaves from the floral wrapping paper. Look for flowers with stems and cut spare unused stems and leaves – both of which can be reshaped – as well as buds, butterflies and two or three fine, long trailing stems for a natural effect.

12. When you have a good pile of cut-outs in front of you, build up the picture on the urn gradually, attaching each cut-out to the surface of the fireboard with a little piece of reusable adhesive. This allows the cut-outs to be applied with the fireboard standing upright, which ensures a more realistic design and makes overlaying cut-outs simpler. When you have finished your initial planned design, step back from the board to look at it. Any gaps will then become obvious, and can be filled with a small bud or leaf as necessary.

13. When you are completely satisfied with the design, carefully chalk around the outside edges of the cut-outs, to mark their shape on the board. This is essential with an overlaid design, indicating where the motifs should be replaced, when you come to remove them one by one for pasting.

14. Gather together the items needed for pasting. Begin with the simplest underneath pieces, taking them one at a time, from the outside edge, and gradually work towards the centre of the design. Once a piece is removed for pasting, chalk around the pieces newly revealed. Remove the bits of reusable adhesive, turn the cut-out upside down and place it on the pasting board. Brush paste carefully over the paper, working from the centre of each cut-out outwards, spreading it evenly over the entire surface and making sure the edges are covered.

15. Lift each piece off the board, using the craft knife if necessary for smaller, more delicate pieces. Replace the paper motifs within

the chalk marks on the board. Working from the middle of each cut-out outwards, smooth the paper down on to the surface, eliminating air bubbles and excess paste with your fingers, and dipping these in a little water from time to time so that there is less likelihood of tearing the paper. Be certain each cut-out is flat before firmly pressing down the edges.

Rinse your fingers occasionally when they become sticky or they might remove the print from the surface of the paper. If you tear a stem, you may be able to lift it off the surface with the craft knife. If not, cut another similar piece, shaping it to mask the error. If a flower has torn, all is not lost – simply stick a butterfly over it!

Hold the fireboard up to catch the light, which will show up any air bubbles and unstuck edges. Tuck a small brush smeared with a little paste under any edges that need resticking and press down firmly. Once the design is complete, leave to dry before cleaning up with a damp sponge or kitchen paper.

16. Adjust the highlighting paintwork on the urn if necessary. Touch up small areas with paint to make good. Leave the paintwork to dry.

17. Wipe the decoupaged surface carefully with the tack cloth to remove dust. Unstuck edges will lift now so restick

them as necessary and press down. Wipe the whole surface of the fireboard with the tack cloth prior to varnishing.

18. Now apply the acrylic lacquer, which has a white, slightly fluorescent look to it when first applied, to the decoupage. Always brush the lacquer outwards over edges, to avoid the brush catching. Apply the lacquer to the whole surface. Leave to dry.

19. Remove dust from the fireboard with a tack cloth before applying more lacquer. Once two or three coats have been applied and have dried you will be able to apply the lacquer more liberally, always brushing it out evenly. Apply as many coats as your time and patience will allow – no less than five to protect all your hard work; 10–15 coats would be better and would give more depth to the finished fireboard.

Regency desk

Originally a 1950s mahogany dressing table, the curved drawers and elegant sweep of the legs added to the appeal of this piece and suggested a Regency-style desk. A simple elegant design of hand-painted leaf swags, little gilded bows and a central oval-shaped motif all add to the desk's charm.

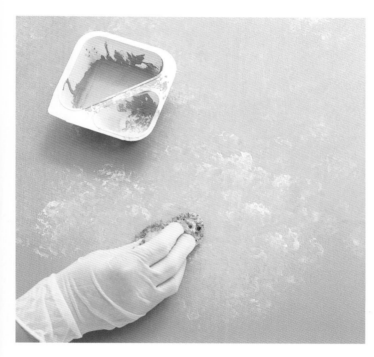

White spirit
4–5 cut-out roses, buds and
    leaves from a good-quality
    wrapping paper
Ready-mixed wallpaper paste
Pasting brush
Pasting board
Good-quality semi-matt
    oil-based varnish or
    polyurethane lacquer
Good-quality clear beeswax
    furniture polish
Soft cloth

The dressing table originally had a fixed back with two upright supports, which held a triple mirror. The original back was replaced with another one cut from ½in (15mm) Medium Density Fibreboard (MDF) in gracefully flowing lines. Once the mahogany "superstructure" was removed, the ply backboard was cut straight across the back, 3in (7.5cm) down, to remove the top section, and the new shaped back firmly screwed to the body of the piece. The pretty drawer handles were removed (and retained) and all the flat surfaces, including drawer fronts, were carefully sanded with a power sander. The legs and curved drawer were sanded by hand.

1. Ensure the surfaces are dust-free – use a vacuum or damp cloth to remove all traces.

2. Using an old paintbrush, apply a coat of shellac varnish to the desk, diluted with a little methylated spirits if it feels too thick. This will prevent dark stain in the wood seeping into the new paintwork (see page 7). Let the shellac dry before applying a second coat.

3. Dilute white acrylic primer undercoat with a little water and give the desk two coats of undercoat, letting the first coat dry before applying the second. Brush on the paint, always working in the same direction as the grain in the wood; watch for a build-up of paint on edges. Leave to dry.

4. Using fine sandpaper, sand all the surfaces carefully, paying particular attention to the edges and surface of the new MDF back, which will have roughened up after the application of paint.

5. Paint the whole piece in the darker turquoise background colour, allowing the first coat to dry before applying a second.

You will need

Shellac varnish and old paintbrush
Methylated spirits
Similar desk, already stripped,
    handles removed and set aside
White acrylic primer undercoat
1in (2.5cm) household paintbrushes
240 grade fine cabinet paper or
    sandpaper
Matt emulsion paint in turquoise
    and very pale turquoise
Plastic cartons
Old spoon

PVA glue
Small natural sea sponge
Kitchen paper
Lightweight gloves
White chalk
Scrap paper
Jam jars with lids
Artist's acrylic tube paint in
    Hooker's green, Payne's
    grey, white, gold and raw
    umber
No. 2 or 3 artist's paintbrush
Artist's oil tube paint in
    raw umber

6. Make up an emulsion glaze in a plastic carton, using two tablespoons of the background turquoise, two tablespoons of PVA glue and up to four parts water. Mix thoroughly. Spoon a little of the paler turquoise into another carton.

7. Squeeze out the sea sponge in clean water to soften it, then squeeze it a second time in kitchen paper to remove excess water. Wearing lightweight gloves, dip the tip of the sponge into the emulsion glaze, then into the pale turquoise. Sponge the surface of the desk all over, turning the sponge as you work to avoid a regimented look and leaving the background colour showing through (see picture, page 127). When the sponge needs replenishing, always dip it into the glaze first, then into the paler colour. The paint finish should be subtle. Remember to sponge underneath and behind

the legs of the desk, too. Ensure the drawers are shut to sponge them and the surrounding frame, then ease them out as soon as you have finished so that they do not stick when the paint dries. When the whole desk is done, leave to dry completely and wash out the sponge in water or the PVA glue will make it rock hard.

8. Replace the drawer handles since it is easier to get a balanced design with these in place.

THE HAND-PAINTED DESIGN: LEAVES, BOWS AND TWISTED RIBBON

9. To mark out the leaf swags, make a chalk mark in the centre back of the desk. Work outwards from the centre, either following the shape of the back board, as here, or dividing the back into equal measurements. Chalk vertical lines to indicate where

each swag begins and ends. These will also mark the positions of the hanging leaves. Chalk out an oval shape freehand.

10. It is best to practise painting the leaves (and later the bows) on paper first. Using a jar lid as a palette, squeeze out on to it a little Hooker's green, Payne's grey and white acrylic tube paint.

The trick of shading leaves is to use a two- or three-colour technique – dark colour on one side of the brush, white on the other. With a wet no. 2 or 3 artist's paintbrush, mix a little of the green and grey paints together, using more green than grey. Wipe one side of the brush on the side of the lid to flatten it, then dip it into the white paint. Place the side tip of the brush on the surface with light pressure and paint a short fine line. Then, with a little more pressure, make a small stroke using the tip of the brush in a slight flicking movement which will form the point of the leaf, releasing all pressure as you do so. Replenish the brush with paint then begin the next leaf with the fine stem line, continuing as before; add another leaf and so on.

Paint the leaves on the back of the desk, then mark the drawers with vertical chalk lines in the centre over the handles, and about ½in (1.5cm) from the edges of the drawers for the leaf swags. The curved centre drawer has four swags. Paint these leaves in the same way.

11. The bow and ribbons use the same shading technique but this time there are only two colours. The trick is to paint the loops and tails in separate sections to give the twisted ribbon appearance.

Fill a jam jar with water and squeeze a little gold and raw umber acrylic paint on to the lid. Mix a little of the two colours together first with some water. Wipe the no. 2 or 3 brush on the edge of the lid, dip it into the raw umber, turn it over, dip the other side of the brush into the gold. Do not overload the brush.

The two main loops of the bow are each painted in three sections. Start with the right-hand loop painting the upper curve first: start from the centre of the bow, working outwards, and place the narrow tip of the brush on to the surface. Make a narrow, short fine line as before, then make a brushstroke by pressing down on to the surface, in an outward and upward movement, stopping just after the top of the first curve. Remove the brush from the work, replenish it with paint and begin again at the centre with the fine line on the lower curve. Sweep the brushstroke out and round to beyond the bottom of the lower curve and stop. Dipping into the colours again, start the third stroke from the end of the second line, pressing then releasing, to join up with the end of the first line, in the middle of the bow – thereby completing the right-hand loop. Paint the

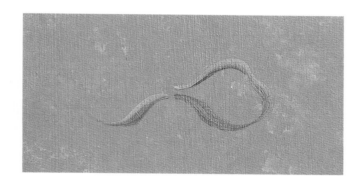

left-hand loop of the bow in the same way then make the smaller top loop in two or three stages as well, finishing with a brush mark in the centre for the knot. Complete the bow by painting the horizontal tails to the sides.

12. Chalk the tiny bows and ribbons above the leaf swags first, before painting them using the same techniques.

13. With the fine sandpaper, distress the desk by rubbing the top edges of the drawers, the side edges, patches under the handles, and where the drawers would be pushed in, as well as on the top surface in areas that would logically be most worn. Remove the dust.

14. To age the desk, make up and apply antiquing liquid made of raw umber oil tube paint and white spirit, following the instructions on page 10. Dilute the colour if it seems too dark. Leave the antiquing liquid on for about 5 minutes, less in hot weather, then start removing it from the decorated and top surfaces first with kitchen paper. Leave it in the little nooks and crannies where dust would have collected over the years. Work until the paper is clean. The antiquing liquid gives the furniture a lovely soft, aged appearance and knocks the newness of the colour back. It will also show up the distressing. Leave to dry overnight without touching since any fingermarks will show up.

15. Stick in place the decoupage decoration (see pages 84–85 for the technique). Once the decoupage is cleaned up and dry, apply a coat of semi-matt oil-based varnish or polyurethane lacquer and leave to dry.

Apply a second coat the next day, or after about 6 hours if the first coat is dry. In two or three days the piece can be waxed with clear beeswax furniture polish and polished with a soft cloth.

Ingenious ideas

Paint old picture frames in vibrant colours, adapt a rustic cupboard or refurbish old chairs – just some of these unique ideas designed for the greatest impact with the minimum of effort!

Queen Anne cabinet

This little cabinet is "wrapped" in fabric depicting a Renaissance design and has been finished with braid and tassels for a stunning effect.

Once a kidney-shaped white wood dressing table, it was fitted with a metal curtain track for fabric, which concealed the drawers beneath. It was riddled with woodworm but had four uneaten legs of solid wood. The overall shape was elegant and its potential was obvious.

The kidney-shaped top was replaced by a close-fitting rectangle of Medium Density Fibreboard (MDF). The woodworm was treated and the old handles discarded. The piece was then sanded well and given two coats of matt emulsion paint in terracotta pink, to match the background colour of the fabric.

The fabric was cut out in sections as follows: the top, two drawer fronts, a wide strip above the top drawer, narrow strips for beneath each drawer, two side strips for the front, two square pieces for the inset side panels and narrow side strips, plus four strips as "bandages" for the legs. The fabric was not measured as such, but was held up against the cabinet for a good pattern match.

The wooden knobs on the drawers were painted to match then screwed back in place through the fabric. The fabric and the braid on the drawers and legs were hot-glued with a glue gun. The final inspirational touch was the use of lovely large key tassels. To protect the top from spills and dust, it would be sensible to have a piece of plate glass cut to fit the top.

Edwardian washstand

Washstands similar to this Edwardian one frequently turn up at auction sales. Made from mahogany, this particular one had a loose, cracked marble top, which has been replaced with a top cut from MDF, and has been given a pretty back to add more interest and detail to the piece.

Treated to an ochre sponged paint finish, the old mahogany and new MDF pieces blend together beautifully. Had the washstand been antiqued and craquelured (see page 11), the new MDF additions would be even less obvious – apparent only to a very discerning eye!

A similar paint finish to this one can be found on pages 82–84, and the detailed technique for painting the twisted ribbons and bows is to be found on pages 128–129.

This charming little cupboard would prove both useful and attractive in a bedroom, bathroom or dressing room.

Edwardian picture frames

These two frames were a very good bargain although the green one was originally a damaged, inside wooden moulding and mount from a larger picture frame. Matching replacement mouldings are available in plastic and can be easily masked by the paint or gilding.

This vibrant blue frame with gilded mouldings is of superb quality. When it was discovered, it was originally in sombre ebonized black wood and held the portrait of an extremely dour-looking Edwardian gentleman, who almost certainly would have deterred prospective buyers who may not have seen the frame's potential!

The heavy-boarded backing, along with peeled grimy paper and years of dust and dirt were removed, and then the frame was given a good wash. When dry, it was given two coats of white polish (shellac varnish would have been another option) and left to dry.

This was then followed by two coats of bright blue matt emulsion paint – similar to ultramarine blue tube paint in colour – which looks particularly good against the gilded moulding. Bevelled mirror glass, ¼in (6mm) thick, has been inserted and the new replacement backing for the wooden frame is made of suitable lightweight plywood.

Bread bin

Old enamel bread and flour bins can often be purchased from second-hand shops, antique markets or from dealers who specialize in tinware. Take care when choosing one since the interior needs to be rust-free, otherwise it will have to be painted with rust-retardent, and this will contaminate any food put inside!

Round bins are more unusual, and this one particularly so as it has holes in the enamel – presumably to stop the bread turning mouldy. Now decorated in a simple, fresh squared design in sage green and white matt emulsion paint, this bin would look good in any kitchen.

French cafetières

These two old white, fluted, enamel coffee pots were purchased while travelling in France. To retain their rustic charm, it was decided to leave them white and they were given a hand-painted design using enamel paints, which were "cooked" in a domestic oven to fix the paint.

The pair can be used just as they are and are dishwasher-proof, too.

Fish kettle

A white enamel fish kettle has been rejuvenated by the use of matt emulsion paints on top of a base coat of red oxide metal primer. The design comprises soft stripes of pink against a lavender background, with a hand-painted motif of lavender and old-fashioned pinks set inside a cameo.

The container looks great displayed on a country dresser or you could remove the lid and fill it with fresh lavender, heady-scented old-fashioned pinks or sweet bergamot from the garden. Alternatively, three plant pots will sit beautifully inside, allowing you to display pink geraniums or other favourite flowers.

Douchepots

Two French enamel douchepots have been transformed into wall-hanging planters for the house or garden. One has an up-to-the-minute design of stripes and checks, the other has a more traditional finish, sponged with soft ochre (see pages 82–84) and painted with a simple leaf design (see pages 128–129).

Such douchepots must be washed thoroughly with a cream cleaner then dried before painting. Two coats of red oxide metal primer need be applied, followed by two coats of acrylic primer undercoat – the addition of a drop or two of washing-up liquid helps if the acrylic paint will not adhere. Finally, two or more coats of an emulsion top colour finish off the douchepots. An alternative for white enamel pots in good condition is to paint them with enamel paints which are fixed by oven "cooking".

If hung outside, trailing plants look great in these planters, while herbs look and smell good and are useful outside a kitchen window or door. Inside the house, such wall-mounted planters are good where space is limited and can be filled with dried flowers.

Galvanized laundry bowl

An old laundry bowl looks smart in fresh stripes of sage green and buttermilk in matt emulsion, decorated with hand-painted mouthwatering red cherries that look good enough to eat, painted with acrylic tube paints. Fill the bowl with cherries or apples, dried flowers or fir cones, or simply stand it on a lovely old dresser where it can be admired as a purely decorative piece.

Lloyd Loom chairs

What an attractive scene: three comfortable wicker chairs, filled with soft downy cushions and pulled up under the shade of the trees on a hot sunny day. These are an invitation to sit down and relax and to wait for the tea tray or cool drinks to arrive.

Three shabby old chairs, which had been overpainted many times during their lives, are now painted in matt emulsion in these cheerful colours of foxglove pink, purple and soft sea green, and have found a new role in a country garden. To revamp an unspoilt wicker chair or to smarten up a new one, spray painting is preferable to avoid clogging up the weave.

Measurements

*Both imperial and metric measurements
have been given throughout this book.
When following instructions, you should
choose to work in either imperial or
metric, never mix the two. Below is a
quick reference conversion chart for use
when buying and working with fabrics,
while to the right, conversion rulers
provide an easy checking aid.*

FABRIC LENGTHS

1/8yd	=	10cm	3³/₄yd	=	3.5m
1/4yd	=	20cm	4yd	=	3.7m
3/8yd	=	40cm	4³/₈yd	=	4m
1/2yd	=	45cm	4¹/₂yd	=	4.2m
5/8yd	=	60cm	5⁷/₈yd	=	4.5m
3/4yd	=	70cm	5yd	=	4.6m
7/8yd	=	80cm	5¹/₂yd	=	5m
1yd	=	1m	10yd	=	9.2m
1¹/₂yd	=	1.4m	10⁷/₈yd	=	10m
2yd	=	1.9m	20yd	=	18.5m
2¹/₄yd	=	2m	21¹/₃yd	=	20m
2¹/₂yd	=	2.3m			

FABRIC WIDTHS

2³/₄yd	=	2.5m
3yd	=	2.7m	36in	=	90cm
3¹/₄yd	=	3m	44/45in	=	115cm
3¹/₂yd	=	3.2m	48in	=	120cm
			60in	=	150cm

1in = 2.54cm
(2.5cm approx)

3ft = 1yd
= 1m (approx)

1cm = 0.3937in
(³/₈in approx)

1m = 3.281ft

1ft = 0.3048m

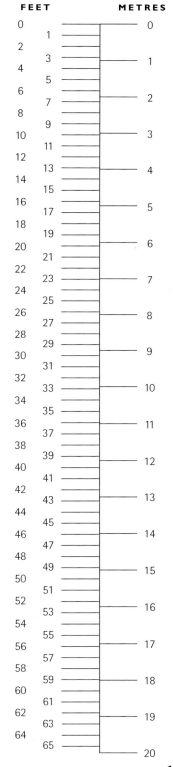

Directory of suppliers

Pearl Paint
Pearl Paint Home Decorating Center
58 Lispenard Street
New York, NY 10013
212-431-7932   x4530
www.pearlpaint.com
New York's premier selection of products for artists and home decorators.

Bristow & Garland
45-47 Salisbury Street
Fordingbridge
Hants SP6 1AB
UNITED KINGDOM
01425-657337
Antiquarian booksellers, also corbels, urns and plinths, cherubs and masks, as well as lovely antique prints and quality gifts.

Brodie & Middleton Ltd
68 Drury Lane
London WC2B 5SP
UNITED KINGDOM
0171-836-3289
Decorating brushes, paints, pigments, powder colours, metallic powders etc.

Caxton Decorating & Interiors
26-30 Salisbury Street
Fordingbridge
Hants SP6 1AF
UNITED KINGDOM
01425-826429
Everything for decorating and DIY. Curtain piles of every type and interesting clips and fixtures, tassels, cords and huge range of fabrics by fast-ordering service. Interior design service.

Craig & Rose plc
172 Leith Walk
Edinburgh EH6 5EB
UNITED KINGDOM
0131-554 1131
Extra pale dead-flat varnish, gold leaf, gold size, paint manufacturer with stockists throughout the UK.

Earth Guild
33 Haywood Street
Asheville, NC 28801
1-800-327-8448
Materials, tools, and books for handcrafts including dyes and pottery.

Modern Options
2325 Third Street
Suite 341
San Francisco, CA 94107
415-252-5580
Extensive collection of finishing products that create authentic antique finishes.

Green & Stone
259 King's Road
London SW3 5ER
UNITED KINGDOM
0171-352 0837
Artist's materials – acrylic varnish, crackle varnish, shellac varnish.

Michael's (Many locations throughout the US)
Castle Ridge Shopping Center
410 Street Route 10
East Hanover, NJ 67936
973-887-3024
www.michaels.com
Various arts and crafts supplies.

Rubena Grigg
Telegraph Cottage
Cranborne
Dorset
BH21 5QU
UNITED KINGDOM
Tel/Fax 01725-517826
Courses in large garden studio at the author's home in decoupage, painting furniture, antique finishes and craquelure, decorative paint finishes and trompe l'oeil. Brochure available on request.

C. Harrison & Son
High Street
Fordingbridge
Hants SP6 1AS
UNITED KINGDOM
01425-652376
Artist's materials, office supplies, gift wrap – some ideal for decoupage.

Flax Art & Design
1699 Market Street
San Francisco
CA 94103
415-552-2355
www.flaxart.com

Mendel's Art Supplies
1556 Haight Street
San Francisco,
CA 94117
415-621-1287

Belcaro Paint Decorating Center
830 South Colorado Blvd.
Denver, CO 80246
303-757-5435

Liberon Waxes Ltd
Mountfield Industrial Estate
Learoyd Road
New Romney
Kent TN28 8XU
UNITED KINGDOM
01797-367555
Patinating waxes for verdigris and bronze, large range of gilt creams in metal, silver, silver gilt and several golds, white polish, liming wax etc. Available in small quantities.

LIBERON PRODUCTS FROM:
Sepp Leaf Products
Suite 1301
381 Park Avenue South
New York
NY 10016
212-683 2840
A comprehensive range of products for the artist and home decorator.

Malabar
31-33 South Bank
   Business Centre
Ponton Road
London SW8 5BL
UNITED KINGDOM
Tel: 0171-501 4200
Fax: 0171-501 4210
Suppliers of fine cotton and silks.

MALABAR FABRICS FROM:
Davan Industries
144 Main Street
Port Washington
NY 11050
516-944 6498

Polly Mobsby
(see Bristow & Garland, UNITED
KINGDOM, Tel: 01425-657337)
Fine textiles, antique linen and
lace, also antique pine furniture.

John Myland Ltd
80 Norwood High Street
West Norwood
London SE27 9NW
UNITED KINGDOM
0181-670 9161
Artist's brushes, huge range of
wax polishes (antiquing waxes in
different colours, liming and
patinating waxes), lacquers,
shellac varnish and white polish,
earth colours, pigments and dyes.

Fabric Bonanza
350 Karin Lane
Hicksville, NY 11801
516-681-0505
www.fabricbonanza.com
Chain specializing in fabrics, arts
and crafts, home decorating and
florals.

NOUVEAU FABRICS FROM:
1734 Tully Circle N.E.
Atlanta
GA 30329
4-0463 3266

Osborne & Little
90 Commerce Road
Stamford
CT 06902
203-359 1500

Polyvine Ltd
Vine House
Rockhampton
Berkeley
Glos GL13 9DT
UNITED KINGDOM
01454-261276
Environmentally safe water-
based products, decorator's
acrylic varnishes and lacquer
suitable for decoupage, huge
range of decorating materials,
including shellac varnish and
white polish, and bronzing liquid
in small quantities.

Polyvine Inc.
27825 Avenue Hopkins
Unit 1, Valencia, CA 91355-4577
As above.

Revival Upholstery
89 Purewell
Christchurch
Dorset BH23 1EJ
UNITED KINGDOM
Inspired upholstery ideas,
curtains and fabrics.

Star Supplies
P O Box 86
Mendocino, CA 95460
707-937 0375

Stone the Crows
3-5 Broad Street
Bath
Avon BA1 5LJ
UNITED KINGDOM
01225-460231
Mexican handmade furniture,
decorative gifts, household
accessories, Italian china etc.

Wallpaper Imports
311 Route 46
Fairfield, NJ 07004
Tel: 973-882 8180
Fax: 973-882 0168

www.artstores.com
Discount art materials and
supplies on the Internet.

Zebedee Fabrics
120 Seabourne Road
Southbourne
Bournemouth BH5 2HY
UNITED KINGDOM
01202-422811
Huge selection of fabrics, braids,
tassels and upholstery supplies
in stock.

Index

Acknowledgements

This book is for Amelia and Mark Robinson, with my love.

First I want to thank Peter and James for building the wonderful studio, making it possible for me to do this book - I love it. My special thanks to my son James for his endless patience and for being such a "wiz" with the jigsaw. His vision and many inspirational ideas transformed mundane, often decrepit bits of furniture into the most stunningly, stylish pieces. Well done!

I am indebted to the following people: Di Lewis, for her inspired photography throughout the book and her kindness and encouragement, speed and sense of humour, all of which made even the step-by-step shots pleasurable! Kirsty Craven, Stylist, for her hard work and moral support. Barbara Latham, for her wonderfully de-stressing aromatherapy massages, which kept me going. Belinda Ballantine for teaching the worst student the basics of gilding (I will be back!). Katey Spratt, Revival Upholstery, for her super work and for pulling all the stops out. Dale, Jenny, Rosalee and Sue at Caxton Decorating & Interiors, for their ongoing help, advice and fun. John Zebedee for all his help, bringing braid, tassels and fabrics home to save me time. My friend, Polly Mobsby, for the medieval chair and other props for the photographs. Richard Paintner for allowing me to use his beautiful hand-painted roses on the headboard, page 110.

The following companies generously donated fabrics for several projects, which greatly enhanced the book and for which I am most grateful: Crowson Fabrics, for the delightful Victorian-style fabrics on pages 95, 99 and 133; Malabar, the sumptuous Suliman silks on pages 58 and 115 and Nouveau Fabrics, the gorgeous Charleston Renaissance-style fabric on pages 72 and 132.

The following companies kindly loaned items for the book, for which I thank them: Caxton Interiors, for the voile on page 47; Leekes of Melksham, for the pedestal and basin on page 68; Stone The Crows, for the sailing boat on page 68; Indigo, for the lovely antique porcelain handles on page 100; The Compasses Inn, Damerham, Hampshire for allowing us to use their lovely garden for the shot on page 25.

I would also like to thank Barbara Latham for her lovely work on the French enamel bathroom set, page 68. Lastly, Nina Sharman, Senior Editor at Hamlyn, Louise Griffiths, Designer, and my Editor, Jo Lethaby, for her good-natured quiet patience, while painstakingly editing my rambling text!